MW00325401

Mark My Love

A MEMOIR

JENNIFER M. ALEMANY

Mark My Love is a work of nonfiction.
Some names and identifying details have been changed.

Copyright © 2020 by Jennifer M. Alemany

All rights reserved. No part of this publication may be reproduced,
distributed, or transmitted in any form or by any means, including
photocopying, recording, or other electronic or mechanical
methods, without the prior written permission of the publisher,
except in the case of brief quotations embodied in critical reviews
and certain other noncommercial uses permitted by copyright law.
For permission requests, write to the author, addressed
"Attention: Permissions" at jennifer@jennifermalemany.com.

For more details visit:
www.jennifermalemany.com

Ordering Information:
For details, contact jennifer@jennifermalemany.com.

Print ISBN: 978-1-09835-452-7
eBook ISBN: 978-1-09835-453-4
Printed in the United States of America on SFI Certified paper.
First Edition

This book is dedicated to the memory of my mother, Elizabeth Ann Luna.

Life isn't about waiting for the storm to pass.
It's about learning how to dance in the rain.

—VIVIAN GREENE

CONTENTS

INTRODUCTION

K nowing the life that I have lived so far, some have said I defied my cultural Latin background, or as I like to say I'm just living the life I want! So those of you out there who know the pressures of your community and your family—there is a way to make it through and without any of the guilt. I'm living proof.

My life is absolutely nothing like I thought it would be when I was younger. I remember wanting a huge family. The kind where all the cousins grew up to be close, kinda like my family, or at least what it used to be. I set out to be an early-childhood teacher: I was going to make a difference with young kids and their families. I was sorta on the way to a version of the family and life I wanted. Then as we all know, life had something else in store for me, and I went with the flow.

Here I am forty-six years old, single, living with my puppy Leo and embarking on a writing adventure. If someone had told me this would be my life, I would have been literally on the floor laughing. I can't speak for anyone else, but when you are in your midforties and you are riding the waves of life, you would think it's not the time to shake things up and play pick-up sticks. Life has thrown me some major curve balls at this point, and I did what I could to get through them. Know that life will try to get you down. It's up to you to keep things moving along. So maybe it was the time to embark on a new chapter of sorts. You can start anything new at any given moment. You don't need permission from anyone. You just need that fire in your belly to start doing what your heart desires. You do have the strength and power to change the course of your life. Do something you haven't done before. Notice how you feel afterward. Do life with joy: nothing else matters.

Our culture is what makes us who we are; who we become is up to us. I did life the way it wanted me to, instead of doing it the way others wanted me to. It takes bravery, perseverance, and a sense of humor. Once you start doing your own thing like I did, you'll hear a lot from those around you, whether it be praise, being told how they would have done it, the yes you did the right thing or an array of other colorful commentaries. Take them all lightly. People are who they are. An exciting new thing can be fun for many in your life, and it's their way of enjoying some of it, too. And think about the new cultural traditions you could be bringing into your community. What an amazing example you could set for the next generation! We all have the gift to blaze new trails: your adventure could be in a history book some day, you never know. Don't take that future from young people everywhere.

My story will be familiar to some and different to others. That's how I wanted it be: I make a point to surround myself with different people whether it be generationally, genderwise, and/or culturally. It makes for a much more interesting life. My true hope is to enlighten just anyone with my memories. Life is never easy, but when you hear someone speak of something that you are going through and how they navigated it, there is some ease of mind. It doesn't mean you have the answer now, it just means you could exhale for one moment knowing someone has felt what you are feeling. I continue to do the best I can with what I am given in life; you are doing the same, so give yourself some credit, give yourself a break, LOVE yourself.

P.S. Excuse some of my colorful language throughout my story—it's how I speak sometimes, and I wanted to be true to you and to me.

CHAPTER ONE

Jenny from the Block

L ove is such a complex thing, when you think about it. It is one of the first things most of us experience upon arriving into this world. It takes on different forms in our lives, and we start to learn that there are so many dimensions to it. Soon enough we also learn about losing love and feeling all the heartache through a broken heart. I have been blessed to know all kinds of love in my life and have also survived losing love. I'm genuinely thankful for all the experiences because it has all brought me to the life of joy and gratitude that I live now. All the pain brought me clarity and put everything into perspective. Through a tunnel of darkness, I discovered profound light at the other end, and I decided to share a piece of my journey with my community.

I've never been one to go into some long, drawn-out story about my childhood and how it molded everything in my life as it stands today. Understand, I believe that the effects of one's childhood greatly impacts everything; I just don't need to go on and on about it, so I'll be keeping it short and sweet. I'm a strong believer in less is more. Have you ever asked yourself who you really are? Shit, who the hell am I? I guess I should start there.

I'm Jennifer Maria from Brooklyn, New York, born and raised, and it's in my blood. I lived predominantly in the Sunset Park and Bay Ridge area for most of my life. Brooklyn will always be a part of my soul no matter where I end up. I'm the Brooklyn girl who makes sure to tell people that is where I'm from, it's not just *the city*, it's very different. I also pride myself in knowing a good bagel and really good pizza. It comes with the territory, coming from the hood and all. You see the Brooklyn of today, 2019, is not the Brooklyn I grew up in during the '70s, '80s, '90s and onward…

The '70s Brooklyn I remember were the days where we lived in a three-family home owned by a relative, all trying to make ends meet. All middle-class families lived on the block, mostly Irish-American, Italian, and Puerto Rican. If you walked a few blocks from the old hood, you would find yourself in the middle of the Hasidic Jewish community. It all seemed like everyone did their best to get along. I can still picture the eclectic mix of people I would see when I was out and about with my mother. I would say the '80s weren't that much different as far as the hood was concerned. Everyone was just moving with the ages: there were roller-skating rinks, neon-colored clothing, a lot of hair spray and, if you had some money, Jordache jeans, too. Damn, I remember that I wanted a horse on my jean pockets just like all the pretty girls… I don't remember anyone in my Latin circle having those jeans. As the decades went on, other families started to move in. Mexican-American, Asian-American, and Indian-American. The faces somewhat changed, but it was still a festive stew of amazingly culturally different people, it was great to grow up in such a diverse environment. The mom-and-pop shops surrounded us, and there was the small newspaper store, and the candy shop with buckets filled with five-cent treats. Brooklyn used to be the place where everyone knew the other families, and they all watched out for each other. Today, it's a trendy borough that is expanding rapidly and losing its old-school soul. That soul is a part of me and the memories I have.

I'm the youngest of four daughters raised by a single mom. There is a nine-year difference between me and the eldest. My mother's first marriage ended after a few short years; then she met my father. And my parents had a great love affair, but that wasn't enough to keep it together. My father decided to leave when I came along, bottom line. My mother loved my father very much, and it was evident in how she spoke of him: she never said a bad word about him, she could never do it. Hell, I egged her on to call him some colorful names when I was in my teen years; it didn't happen. I just wanted to see that she was pissed that he left. My father wasn't in my life at all. I just share his last name and genetics. I learned more about my father after his death, to be quite honest. I come from Latin roots. My maternal grandmother was from Arecibo, Puerto Rico; my maternal grandfather was from Veracruz, Mexico; and my father was from Cuba. My mom was what they call a Nuyerican. A Nuyerican is specifically a Puerto Rican born in New York City. She taught us all Spanglish for sure! Some would say that all of this makes up the *caliente* that is in my blood. I'm a Puerto Rican, Mexican, Cuban-American and proud of it!

We didn't have much growing up since there were five of us as a family. We had each other which was important. My mother did the best she could with what she had, and she always worked very hard. She kept a roof over our heads, clothes on our backs, and food on the table. Things were far from perfect, but the love was always there. She had a joy within her even with all her struggles. I always knew right from wrong because of what she would teach us. She raised us to be moral and walk in God's light. She wanted us all to have a better life, to dream bigger because she'd had nothing growing up and wanted more for her children. I remember Friday nights were all about us getting a pizza and a 64-oz. bottle of Pepsi from Johnny's on Fifth Avenue in Sunset Park, then watching *Dallas* as a family. Those Friday nights were the best thing to me as a kid: we were all together, and all seemed great because of it. That was the treat my mom could give us each week, and it was enough for me! It was such a simple thing; however, it was so impactful to me, and it's a great memory.

Our extended family was always around, aunts, uncles, and all their kids. My aunts and uncles were all interesting folks. By *interesting*, I mean they all looked similar in appearance—dark hair, dark eyes, caramel skin tone—but gave different lessons and messages to us kids. It could get very confusing. After a while you knew who would be the quiet and loving kind, versus the *Don't do any of this in life* type because they knew what the outcome would be for just about any scenario you could create. I remember one conversation with one of my aunts when I was about seventeen years old, and this is where the confusion I spoke of earlier came into play...

We were in the kitchen cleaning up after a family dinner.

"Jenny, listen. I know you are at that age when boyfriends come into the picture. I just need to tell you this piece of advice...a white boy only wants one thing from a young, pretty Latin girl... You understand what I'm sayin'?"

My head was spinning with confusion because some of my cousins were married to white people and their children were white. Plus, another aunt a few months prior to this conversation had asked me if I had a boyfriend, and she went on to tell me that she didn't care if I had a boyfriend, she was more concerned that he was *Spanish-speaking* as she referenced it. Her advice: *Never* get involved with a

Latin man! I think that is when I realized without a doubt that my family was a little screwed up like every other family on the planet. Thank God we were so-called normal! Our cousins were our friends before we had the chance to make real friends. And it worked out because we had such an eccentric group and of all ages, too. There were about sixteen or so first cousins, so you can imagine we had a few badasses, some artists, a sturdy handful of drama queens, the musicians, a small group of good dancers (I'm one and proud! Holla!), and the singers, too. Among that group there were those who were self-proclaimed saints and saviors but only on Sundays and other holy days. And, if you didn't fit into those exact categories, you may have had a little bit of everything. It was fun—what can I say? It was a total, fucking circus most of the time! Our family was the core of a lot of my childhood memories. I thought it was great to have a large family: there was always someone to hang out with. I was the youngest grandchild, and it was interesting being the youngest all the way around. It wasn't the greatest when I was a kid since I couldn't do a lot, but as I got older I started to learn lessons from my older cousins, which helped me throughout my life. My grandmother had such a spunk to her, too, and all the grandchildren got a glimpse of it at different times.

I have a memory of going to the bank with Grandma when I was about five years old. My grandmother was beautiful. She had shiny white hair that had a glimmer to it like when the sun hits a fresh coat of snow. Her skin always looked fresh like a drop of dew on a red rose petal. She was a strong woman: she had come to the United States from Puerto Rico by herself with only a few dollars to her name. She was the real deal…all five feet zero inches of her! We were in line when a lady got in front of us.

My grandmother said in a soft voice to the lady, "Excuse me, there is a line here," pointing to us and all the folks behind us, too.

The woman looked us up and down.

She snapped back, "I was already here, and why don't you go back to your country?"

"We are in our country!" my grandmother rapidly responded.

The woman rolled her eyes, turned back around, and mumbled, "I doubt this is your country."

Next thing I knew, Grandma had lightly hit the lady with her handbag and stormed out of the bank dragging me along with her.

I was giggling because I was surprised and very excited.

I didn't know much about what was behind what had happened. I was too young to realize the ignorance of some and their fear of the unknown. I never knew if my grandmother ever told my mother or any of my aunts what had happened. She may have chosen to keep it to herself. What I did know was that my grandmother was a warrior! That day in the late '70s has always remained with me, and with the time we live in now, it brings tears to my eyes that we are still on the same page.

I went to school in Brooklyn, with the exception of one year in Manhattan. I had good friends in high school, but I couldn't stand school in general. The high school I attended was unique, and we could pick our classes, but I just wanted to learn about what interested me and none of the rest. I wanted to learn about psychology, I wanted to write, and I wanted to take education classes to become a teacher. I thought all the rest was a waste of my time. I lived for the weekends when I could go into the city to stay at my best friend Jasmine's place. Her family was from Puerto Rico, and I loved being around all of them. What I have learned, like with anything, is that we are all different, even within the Latin culture. They made classic dishes just like my family, but they were all unique-tasting. I thought that was the bomb! The *pernil* and *arroz con granules* would melt in my mouth. I felt comfort being surrounded by our culture: it always felt like family, it always felt like home. I never questioned who I was when I was there, and I always had a sense of security. I was always grateful for that safe haven. They were my family without a doubt. What they did share with my family was a strict upbringing all around, and that was the only reason my mother would give me the freedom to stay overnight so far away: if she asked me to be home by seven o'clock in the evening, their rule would be six o'clock, and she loved it! I used to think that it was crazy that I would get excited to go somewhere with even more rules, but I was with my BFF, and that was the only place I wanted to be.

My high-school years molded a lot of who I was to become. I often did what I wanted without minding the group and definitely not following others. I think I came to be that way because I had so many culturally different friends. Not many could say that: everyone stuck to who and what they knew. I walked my own path no matter what. I picked my own style of everything. And with that, I went through all types of phases with my clothing, too. I went through what my mother called the black-pantyhose phase. This was where I was wearing short black skirts, black stockings, and an oversize sweater just about every single day. I remember overhearing part of a conversation my mother was having with her best friend who also had a daughter around my age.

My mom giggled and said, "Well, Jennifer is going through her black-pantyhose phase. Yeah, she gets upset if they aren't the right sheerness. It seems quite intense."

I flayed my arms at her while rolling my eyes. "Do you have to tell her everything that I'm doing?"

"Oh, now she's mad that I shared that with you," she replied and laughed away, disregarding any moment of dramatics I was acting out in front of her. And dramatics it was… I can still picture us during that conversation, typical teenager not wanting to be talked about, and with a boatload of hair spray in my hair…it was '80s!

I went through the baggy-jeans phase, the tight-jeans phase, bodysuits, leggings, all-black clothing, and so much more. I wasn't afraid to do my own thing. And my mother shared all of it with her bestie and my aunts for sure: that's how things were in our Latin family, and everyone got used to it soon enough. I listened to the music that I wanted to regardless of my friends. Gloria Estefan and Miami Sound Machine, Sade, Bon Jovi, and Fleetwood Mac would make up my everyday playlists. Then, I would dabble in some house music and reggae when the feeling came on. I loved all the differences in the music. My taste was all over the place and natural to me. I loved to dance to it all. Their music would touch my soul over and over, I would listen to their words and get goose bumps on my arms. I'm still listening to all those songs today; they will never get old to me. I learned independence during those years. My lack of interest in the common school studies and my lack of desire to fit in began to prove to me that I was unique and that I was strong. I kinda new early on I would be doing my own thing for the duration of time, I didn't see that changing in my life. I liked it; it was refreshing. I always felt older than I really was because of this spirit. I remember it feeling lonely at times in my youth—who is going to understand someone so deep? As I got older I embraced the alone time and realized I needed it, the person I was needed it. I recognized what I needed and claimed it. I had to tell myself that was okay then, and I remind myself that it is okay today. I was a shy girl regardless of what it seemed like at times. This period in my life would mark the beginning of me moving away from my true self and altering who I was to make others (I thought) happy. After a few years of body criticism from others, I began to verse myself in how to put myself down without anyone's help. From about the age of eleven, folks began to start telling me to watch my weight and for different reasons.

"Jenny, be careful what you are eating; the women in our family always have a weight problem." This statement was said to me by a cousin who hadn't really seen the family in a while. Yes, surely you are thinking something similar to what I was: nice comment after not seeing someone in years. I started to log all these remarks in my head and refer back to them a multitude of times in the decades to follow.

Everything else, meaning any part of my external self, would be criticized by those around me, and some not meaning to do it directly, but it would end up that way. My hair was never straight enough or curly enough, another major dilemma. I was too short, then at one point—yes—I was told I was too skinny. So you see, I tore my body apart because everyone told me it wasn't quite right. Hell, I remember my childhood doctor, who was a Latin male, telling my mother after my annual physical that I should start to think about eating less because at some point in my life he figured I would want a boyfriend. Now, I was not more than eleven or twelve years old at the time. My mother didn't say anything to him, she was just listening, but I remember feeling horrible. I remember thinking about how ugly I must have been that he said that. All these things dampened the sprit of my life and would impact every single relationship I would have after that for a very long time. I didn't have many boyfriends in high school, and that was by choice. I had guys asking me out, but I always felt I wasn't ready, or if I sensed their intentions weren't genuine, I would just stay on my own; it seemed like the right thing for me at that time. I often wondered why they would be asking me out most of the time anyway. I didn't see any beauty in myself, not in any way. I could barely stop myself from curling up in a ball anytime I received a compliment. The inner damage had been done, and unfortunately, it was embedded in my core. Plus, during that time in the '90s, the teenage-pregnancy rate was off the charts, I wanted nothing to do with it. I had close friends who had decided to have babies, and it worked out for them, but because I had a young niece, I knew the responsibility—no thanks!

I was content being by myself: I didn't want to get into trouble, and I didn't want to get hurt. I was fine with my experiences at that point in my life. I believed my mom's words of wisdom when it came to love, too. She would tell me that life would bring me many adventures that would be amazing, but that I should just try not to grow up too, too fast. She was the wisest woman I knew, and I trusted her. And if anyone asked me now if I would have changed anything during that period of my life? Absolutely not!

CHAPTER TWO

This Latina Had a Dream

I love who I am, my culture. I always tell everyone exactly what I am because I'm so proud of it. Growing up, I didn't see many girls that looked like me on TV, which became even more important to me as I got older. This is why the *who* in *who I am* became the priority. My mother taught me to be proud of my heritage and to be proud to be a woman. She came from a strong woman, and I see them both as an inspiration. I'm a genuine person, someone who did the best she could navigating the waters of life and what the adventures brought forth. Deciding what to do after high school was a lot. I didn't know if I could handle more rigid, institutionalized learning. And I had no idea what I was going to do if I got a job.

I had a scholarship from the "I Have a Dream" Foundation that would pay most of what I needed. So I decided to take the chance and apply to an early-childhood program to pursue my desire to become a kindergarten teacher. It really was the only thing I honestly saw myself doing because I loved little children and how they learned fascinated me. I went to college in Cobleskill, New York. The State University of New York College of Agriculture and Technology at

Cobleskill, to be exact. It wasn't right after I was done with high school, but soon enough, and when I look back I think being a little older helped me with all of it. If I had been younger I may not have stuck it out. It was a very small town compared to the block back in Brooklyn. I was extremely homesick. I couldn't relate to anyone, there was no one from where I was from living on my floor, and I had absolutely no one there. My first thought was *Will my mother actually kill me if I ask to return home?* No. She loved me too much, it could never be that bad. My next thought jumped to money, of course. I said out loud, "Shit! What if they ask us to pay some of the scholarship money back?" That is when I remember sweating and thinking that it was never going to happen. If I mentioned leaving college, it was going to be a big issue all around. So I decided to write a letter to soften the blow! Hey, what can I say, I was twenty years old.

> *Dear Mom:*
>
> *I made a really big mistake. I thought I would love it here because I loved it so much when I visited. It's just not the same from what I remembered. I haven't met anyone that I click with, everyone is so different and you know that doesn't matter to me, but it seems to matter to those I've met so far. I don't know what to do, but I want to come home. I miss you, and I miss Lauren. Please don't be mad at me. It's just a lot harder than I thought it would be. I love you lots.*
>
> *Hugs and Kisses, Jenny*

My mom called the moment she received the letter. When I heard her voice, I initially wasn't able to tell what she was thinking. My mother asked me to give it a few weeks. She told me life is never easy. I often remember those words, and hearing her say them, they somehow keep me on track when I'm going through stuff. When I look back, I don't think it was just being homesick. I think it was being someone very different in a very different place. No one looked like me, spoke like me, or seemed on any level similar to me. And that's hard, let alone just missing home. I made a few friends, did the best to view everything with open eyes. Some days were difficult, and I just wanted to see my mom as I missed her very much. As we all know the reality of life, just when you think it's so horrible…things start to look up! I met a boy I really liked. We were very different, but that's what made it interesting. He had blond hair and blue eyes and had grown up on a farm with his grandparents. He was tall and I was short. We really didn't have a lot in common at all, but somehow we made each other laugh. I started to actually experience life in Upstate NY just outside of campus, and it was beautiful. I had a different perspective on things. For the record, he was what the world would consider white. I only saw *him*: that was all that mattered. It was hard to listen to other Latino students who I was friendly with say things like it was a shame I was wasted on a white guy and such. I never understood why everyone was so afraid. Blood ran through his veins just like it ran through mine. I knew we were different, but it made us all the more amazing. We fell in love. This was a first true love for me, and it meant so much. My mother could tell I was in love, but she was very afraid. Afraid for my heart; she didn't want her baby to get hurt. As with all the lessons of life, love can be a scary one, too. Victor and I started talking about our life together fairly quickly. We mapped out a full plan of the place we were going to live, how many children we would have, and how we would navigate our families living so far apart in NY. It was all a beautiful dream, and then things started to get real.

It was a Sunday afternoon. Victor and I were just hanging in my dorm room when the phone rang.

"Hello," I said with a bubbly tone.

"Hey, it's me. What ya doing?" It was my cousin Christina.

I replied, "Not much. What's going on?"

She then proceeded to tell me our beloved grandmother had passed away. I started crying the moment I hung up the phone. Victor consoled me, but I just wanted my family, and they were so far away. My grandmother was ninety-two years old and had lived a very long life, but it was still very hard. She had lived through cancer for so long, it seemed like she would always be there. I made arrangements to head back to Brooklyn; I notified my professors and made a plan for Victor to drive me to the bus station the next day. I hugged my mom the minute I walked through the door. She said with a teary voice, "I'm so glad to see you, Jenn. That was the first hug I've gotten." Those words got me even more upset. There was no one around to console my mom: how horrible! I tried to do my best to make things easier for her during that time. I had lost my grandma, but she had just lost her mother. I arrived back at school and reunited with Victor. The next few months would bring changes because of everything that had happened with my grandma. I felt guilty for not seeing her that much during my last break because I was working to pay for my books the next semester. I had no one to talk to about the loss and how much I missed her. I didn't want to burden my mom, and I didn't want her to worry about me. So I dealt with what I was feeling on my own. I started to feel like Victor was pulling away from me at times, and I remember not being sure if it was the situation or something else. And it wasn't like our communication was the greatest, being so young and all. A few short months later while I was at home for the summer, my heart was broken. I never really got a reason why, which was the worst thing to experience at that age, but now I know it never really mattered. I became a stronger person because of what had happened. It made me the person I am today. My mother saw my transformation after that heartbreak. I became more determined in my life, more determined in myself. I returned back from the summer break a different person indeed. In a way, I was colder, I was harder, I was mature.

The phone rang one afternoon shortly after arriving back in Cobyland. I was chillin' with two gals who lived on my floor.

I was laughing when I picked up the phone. "Hello."

"Jenn, it's me," Victor said with a whimpering tone.

My eyes opened wide as I looked at my friends and silently mouthed "It's Victor."

"What do you want?" I snapped.

"Do you hate me? I'm sorry for everything. Do your friends hate me?" He sobbed while muttering out all his words.

"Now, why does all that matter? You made this decision, so I guess you'll have to live with it," I replied coldly.

He barely mustered through "I guess you're right."

"Good-bye, then," I immediately responded.

I didn't want to hear anything else so I just hung up the phone, and that was the last I ever heard from Victor. My college years taught me many many lessons. I wouldn't trade those days for anything. I learned what it was like to be a Latina from the city in a small agricultural town, surrounded by nothing that was familiar to me. I learned what strength I had, being by myself and being so far away from home for the first time. I learned what it was like not to have my mother right next to me like she always had been. I learned the value of listening to different people and how you could grow just by talking with them. I learned that the love you feel is always around you, and you should trust in it when you are at your most vulnerable. I learned that falling in love can be a beautiful thing and very painful at the same time. I learned that being able to pick yourself up is important no matter what has happened. I learned who I was through and through. I will never forget those lessons!

CHAPTER THREE

Sometimes to Get to the End... You Have To Go Back to the Beginning

After my Coby years, I headed back to Brooklyn. I went by way of being a live-in nanny for a year in Mahwah, New Jersey, then I securely planted my seeds back in Brooklyn for the next two decades. And by *securely*, I mean every single angle: I lived in Brooklyn, I worked in Brooklyn, my friends and I hung out in Brooklyn. I don't ever remember saying I didn't want to be in Brooklyn, but this was proof that my entire life was now saturated in everything Brooklyn. I went from being the student who said I was all good just getting my high-school diploma to now attending college at night to complete my bachelor's degree. Go figure. I never thought about it much to be honest. What was the point? I wasn't focused on any particular career. I was working a full-time job, I wasn't looking for a next step at all. I figured at that time I would bring home a paycheck and try to figure things out as I went along. I was no longer big on making huge life plans because I realized that the gods are just laughing at you while you are meticulously putting together all those amazing plans. I once had it all mapped out, down to where I would retire. However, like with so many things, it was washed away with the morning waves. It ended up being another lesson: don't map out too much, have an idea but leave the blueprints out of it because it will all be different.

My years working at Brooklyn College were impactful on my life in so many ways. First off, that job paid for the rest of my bachelor's degree! That never would have happened without it, and it was great because there was no pressure to graduate by a certain time, as you could actually go at your own pace. I started out slow because I was concerned that the boredom of general studies would set in, and I didn't want to lose the momentum that I was feeling. I paced myself well, and it worked out, taking night, weekend, online, and eventually summer courses to finish. I was inspired once I began. I remember thinking that I didn't start out with any intent but it turned into the key I needed for my future. I trekked along, and indeed my degree opened up a door that previously a degree-/paperless me would not have been welcomed through. At Brooklyn College, I started working in the field of human resources, and I was actually good at it. I just happened to be at the right place at the right time. I had taken an exam for an office assistant role the year before. It was a test my mother had insisted I take, so I did. She was worried about my future and what I would become. It really didn't matter to me; I wasn't looking at the future at all. I went for a job fair where you had to line up at the university you preferred to work at. Then, they would run through a rapid interview. It was then decided whether you were chosen or just considered. It didn't matter to me, as I was really only there to please my mother. Brooklyn College decided to hire me, and a new journey started fairly quickly. It made sense years later when I looked back on those days: I was always good with people, so I adapted well. It was an interesting place to be. In all my adventures in the borough of Brooklyn, sometimes you came across people who were stuck in another decade, some folks who just would like to talk about the city, and others who wanted to make it well-known that they were from Brooklyn without a doubt.

It was December, 1999. I started a new job, made some new friends, and things were okay from what I remember. I wasn't looking for a romance nor did I have any interest in dating again just yet. I was content with the day-to-day, so I didn't want to rock the boat in any way. Working at a college gave me the opportunity to meet folks from other places, and that brought a lot of new people into my life. I had become close with a gal from California who had some Mexican roots like me. It was refreshing to meet someone who had a different upbringing and life but shared the same culture. Molly was cool, we had a great friendship, and she would end up introducing me to Ben.

Ben was taking night classes at Brooklyn College, art classes as a hobby, as he already had a bachelor's degree. Ben was nothing like anyone I knew from Brooklyn; he was from the Midwest. He was really smart, had a good sense of humor, and didn't take life too seriously. He was nothing like the guys I would generally be attracted to, the usual dark-hair-and-eyes type. Ben was just exploring life on his own in Brooklyn, and we became friends. The honest truth is I thought he was very attractive, but the vow that I had made to myself was stronger than any attraction. I promised myself that I would not get into a relationship again. I didn't want to get hurt. It had taken me five years to repair my heart from Victor's destruction. I wasn't ready. So, we were strictly friends and knew how to have fun together. It was simple. It was easy. Time passed fairly quickly. We had been good friends for a year and so much had happened to both of us personally. He had lost his father and my mother was beginning to fight for custody of her two young grandchildren with me by her side. Our friendship turned romantic after that year's long journey. We were both twenty-five years old, and we respected and trusted one another. We weren't looking for a massive commitment from each other, but it was always clear we enjoyed being together. That relationship and everything else going on in my life at that time would be the start of so many milestones.

I finished a degree in psychology at night. I enjoyed completing my degree. I was able to take some Latin studies courses, and I absolutely loved all of my psychology classes. I remember some people in my life didn't think I would complete it, but I showed them! There were many hurdles along the way, just like anything else. My mother started caring for her two young grandchildren, and I was there to raise them with her while I was in school. There were a lot of sleepless nights which were followed by working all day and classes to follow at night. I remember thinking I wouldn't make it sometimes because it was so hard.

With so many responsibilities on my plate while trying to make a future for myself, there was many a night that I just wanted to give up. I never did, no matter how bad it got. I was working a full-time day job, a part-time nights and weekend job, and going to school at night, which meant I had no days off. What could I do? I had the weight of my family on my back, I had to keep going or we all would have drowned. That wasn't difficult for a Latin family who never made it past a certain socioeconomic level. I don't think the rest of my extended family knew how bad it was. It's hard for me to even think back on those times. My mother had done so much to get ahead in her life; she just wanted to live comfortably for once and not struggle so much. This reset in her life would reset mine as well. I often felt and still feel like my extended family doesn't help one another as a collective. It is hard to watch because if the family doesn't get it as a family unit, how will we ever get it as a human collective? I was and still am always thankful for the opportunities I have been blessed with and for those who guided me toward paths that would help me in changing the course of my life. If it wasn't for all these things, I would, without a doubt, be a statistic of my background.

Ben had encouraged me to go back to school, to try new things, and he showed me more of the world that I hadn't seen up to that point, the world from the New York City view. He somehow showed me that something beautiful can blossom even when there was so much going on and when I was gasping for my life. That love showed me that maybe I had to plant myself back in Brooklyn where it all had started in order to figure out where my path was actually going. And just like life does, it kinda threw a relationship at me when I wasn't looking for one and when I thought was at the worst time ever. Funny thing is you can't plan when a relationship is going to grow, and our relationship had a solid friendship, so it was easy…until it wasn't. Ben had trouble fully committing one hundred percent of himself to our relationship, and I put in about two hundred percent of myself. Neither of us were to blame: we didn't love ourselves completely, so we never could fully love each other.

If only I had been able to see that at that time, maybe I would have spared us some heartache and time. Ben and I had a fifteen-year relationship. When I look back at all we went through, I don't even recognize both of those people anymore. When things were sweet they were very sweet, and he was my escape from the family drama that had been unfolding around me. I know that drama also added to the strains of our stormy relationship. We had intense love for each other, and we grew up together; there was a lot of history there. There were glimmers of hope on my end over our time with each other. I remember one summer morning, we had to stop at a pharmacy on our way back from a visit to the ER. They had discovered I had some kidney stones. While

Ben watched me doubled over in pain for hours, I saw the concern in his eyes. It was always clear he cared about me.

In the pharmacy, there was an elderly man looking for an item he couldn't find. We were passing by him when he asked us if we saw the product he was looking for. I found the product fairly quickly and responded "Here it is, sir."

"Well look at that." The man smiled, looked at Ben and said, "She's a good one, you know!"

Ben giggled. "Oh, I know, she's a keeper." I raised my eyebrow at him and cracked a slight smile.

I always knew not to show too much happiness because such excitement would scare Ben and push him two steps backward in our relationship. That tango was our defining dance.

My mother was impressed by Ben from the moment she met him, and she would invite him over for dinner from the start of our friendship. She told me once that she could tell he loved me, and she just wanted him to do the right thing by me. As time went on and we both entered our thirties, we lived together, but old insecurities would still be there like the roller-skating scar on my knee from my childhood. We had worked to put our apartment together. As we moved in, he would get the tools out and set things up exactly where we wanted them to be. Ben would always complete something and say "We are almost there, Jenny!" I would respond "And where would that be?" and in his classic, noncommittal way, he would say "Exactly where we need to be."

If he had responded any other way, it would have meant things were way more serious. I had strong love for Ben. The kind of love where you would go live in a box on the street if that was the only way you could be with that person. I wanted to be with him, so I sacrificed just about everything for that love. Many sacrifices that hurt too much to think about. It was too late to realize that I would never have been enough for him. And with the blink of an eye, we lost each other completely.

CHAPTER FOUR

When Death Comes Knocking, No One Wants to Answer

Everything in life passes on. I have spoken of the loss of myself, and now on to physical loss. Death of any loved one or something close to us is hard. It's life-altering, to say the least. Some survive and make it through. Others struggle with it for a lifetime. It inevitably changes you in so many ways. For me, it not only broke my heart into a thousand pieces, but it also crushed my soul, my spirit.

My mother had been my hero ever since I was a little girl. Raising four daughters on her own was a full-time job in itself. She was our sole provider. She was the strongest woman in my life, and no one else has come close. The love she gave me was unconditional. She was my mother, my father, and my best friend. She never expressed how hard things were for her, but I always knew from a very young age, that's why I always wanted to help her. I naturally didn't ask for anything. It's hard to describe how I knew things weren't easy; I just had that gut feeling just like folks always talk about. So I chose to not add to any of her hardships. I just wanted her love and to be near her. Nothing else mattered. I now realize that habit of not asking for things guided the rest of my life. In hindsight, it taught me to silence my voice in every-thing I did. It also clouded my inner voice to what I needed from relationships. I put everyone's needs first, and my needs were nowhere in sight. My mother deserved the world and so much more. She taught me what true love meant. She never judged me, and she told me I was beautiful no matter what. She taught me right from wrong.

She showed me how to be independent and how to follow my heart. When I look back, it occurs to me now that I really didn't have specific dreams of what I wanted to be in life. I was always dancing as a little girl, and I remember dreaming of being a ballerina, yet I never asked about dance class. Up until now, I didn't realize that I pushed most of my dreams aside to help others, and I have no regret in that. It made me stronger, and I truly learned the meaning of being selfless. In time, I would learn to ask for things again. I was the apple of my mother's eye. I made her laugh, and I took her out of her comfort zone with my spirit. We had such a special relationship. She never pushed me, and she gave me space to grow but always kept a watchful eye. I could always feel her love. I always knew love existed because of her. It's hard to explain; I just felt it. I guess that's why I feel sad for others who have never experienced truly unconditional love because I've had it, and it's phenomenal! My life lacked for nothing because of my mother. She taught me about being a strong, classy Latina, which meant respecting myself no matter what; it meant I could do anything that I set my mind to; and it meant standing tall no matter what. I wanted to give her everything I could, and I was working on that when the bottom of life dropped out. And time was no more.

My connection to spirit, to the universe, was always intense and started at a young age. A week before my mother went into the hospital, I had a strong feeling about something. I didn't know what it was, but I had to call her and ask if all her papers were in order in case anything bad happened. I called her immediately from work on that cold February morning in 2008.

"Hi, Jenn. I thought you said you were going to call me later and come by for dinner. What's going on? I was just going to watch one of my novelas."

My mother had taken up watching Spanish novelas during this chapter of her life, something that without a doubt brought her back to times of watching them with my grandmother. It was a happy place in her soul and it made me happy watching that joy in her.

I cut right to the point.

"Mom, are all your papers in order? If not, we should find some time to get started on that." I said in a business tone as if I were making a business transaction, a tone I had never really used with my mother.

"Jenny, why are you talking about this all of a sudden? Is something wrong?" she replied with a concerned yet calm voice.

"No, I just think it's important. If anything was to happen, what would happen with the boys? Let's talk more about it tonight. I love you." I didn't want her to start to worry about anything, so I quashed the conversation.

When I got to her apartment that night, I remember her asking me why I was bringing that up out of the blue. I didn't have an answer to that question because I didn't know. What I did know was that it was important because she was raising her two grandsons, my twin nephews, The Boys. She willingly had taken them in when their mother, her daughter, could not care for them. (I know many of you may wonder what that story is about, but this is my story and the why of that story isn't really relevant. Another tale for another time.) They meant the world to her, and so did her granddaughter. My mother loved all of her family with her heart and soul. She had so many nieces and nephews. Each one was special to her. She had pictures of every one of them in her old photo albums. So there was no doubt that her grandchildren made her light up; however, she was raising kids on her own again, so I dedicated my life to helping her with all of them. I knew if anything happened to her, it would destroy them, and unfortunately that's exactly what went down. She had had a full checkup and was deemed in good health four months prior to her passing away. She was eating better and had lost some weight. Her doctor praised her for doing so well with her health. I think she mentioned him actually giving her a high five during her last visit to his office. However, something had gone terribly wrong. Things moved so quickly that I barely had time to breathe, let alone digest the reality that my mother was dying.

Can you say I was pissed at everything in life, in spirit, and at God? Why would this happen to such a beautiful soul, a great love in my life? Right, that didn't matter because it was happening…and there was nothing I could do to stop it. I went into an automatic state. I didn't express how I was feeling to anyone, just the basics with no details, because to me, what was the point? I had so much on my plate. What was I going to do without her? None of it mattered because there were two little boys to think about plus a young lady who would look to their aunt for support and love. I didn't have the time or energy to think about my own feelings. I was well aware that the rock in my life was slowly passing on, and I would have to become their rock. I didn't want that job at all, but I didn't have many options at the time, and anyway everything was moving rapidly. I silenced my tears and put on the bravest front that I could muster. That took every inch of my body, soul, core, and so much more. The doctors weren't sure what was going on when I brought her into the ER that cold Friday night. So I waited with her there all night long by myself. They took blood and did test after test.

She had lost a lot of blood, and the team of physicians didn't know how or why. One doctor took me aside after a few hours.

"Ms. Alemany, your mother, all her labs are off, way off. We have to run a few more tests, but I have a hunch on what I think it may be," the doctor blurted out rather quickly.

"What do you think it is?" I responded immediately.

"Her sister had Non-Hodgkin Lymphoma, and the tests so far are leaning that way. I'm sorry, this isn't easy for anyone," he said and then looked down at the floor.

"Thank you, Doctor." I quickly walked away and went outside for some air. I decided to bum a cigarette off someone outside. It had been years since I had smoked one but I thought what the hell! I went back inside to my mother's bedside, as she was up from her nap at that point.

"Jenn, where were you? Did the doctors say anything else?" she asked.

I had felt such guilt that she was wondering where I was that I felt selfish quite honestly. I couldn't tell her that I had just had an out of body experience because of what the doctor had told me and had become a walking zombie who went outside for a quick smoke. It didn't seem logical.

"No, all the tests haven't come back yet." I didn't see the point in saying otherwise to her. I figured let all the tests come back, and then we would cross that bridge. That wide, fucking bridge...that long, cold, windy, wide, fucking suspension bridge. Yes, those words describe some of my feelings.

My eldest sister did a brief drive-by and then went on with her own business that evening. I didn't say anything to her because she seemed to be in a rush. She didn't seem to want to be bothered with anything having to do with the situation. It was too much for her. Hell, it was too much for me! I've often wondered why I was the one to take care of things since I'm the youngest, but it all started to make sense. I'm the strongest, I always have been, so I did my due diligence. The hospital finally got her into a room after two days in the ER. When the doctors came to the conclusion that it was cancer, all hell broke loose after that. Some of them had hoped for the best at first, and for a nanosecond, things were looking up. Honestly, I knew it was the end. I sensed her spirit was exhausted, her life was coming to an end.

I was the one to tell her she had cancer, not the doctors. What seemed like the right thing at the time, for me to tell her the diagnosis… When I think back, I shouldn't have been the one to tell her. I had felt pressure from others. I think what happens is everyone thinks about what they would do if it was them, but guess what? They are not you, and you are not them. She cried for only two minutes, barely that. It's the hardest thing in the world to see your hero break down completely. She dried her tears and in her strong voice said "I want to see the boys while I still look healthy. Please arrange to bring them by tomorrow."

I cleared my throat and choked back my tears. "Sure, Mom. Whatever you want."

We talked a lot during her last days. It was barely thirty days from beginning to end. I made sure I told her everything I needed her to hear, no matter how hard it was for me.

"Mama, all those cutting cards I used to get in high school… They weren't mistakes. I barely went to homeroom during freshman year. There, I said it. Phew! Wow, I have been carrying that around for so long, that felt really good to get that out after all these years." I still couldn't look at her while I made that confession because I didn't want her to be mad about it. Funny thing, why would that make her mad at this point in time? It just showed how I never wanted to disappoint her with any of my life decisions.

"Look at what you have become as a person, Jenn. I'm so proud of you. I think I can forgive the cutting cards." She genuinely laughed.

"Thanks, because the guilt of those high-school mistakes have weighed heavy on me." I laughed, but I did mean it. I just didn't like high school.

Some days we laughed at old memories, and some days we cried about them. She just wanted to go home. And what we all thought meant back to her apartment in Brooklyn really meant home to her Creator. Home with her mother, her sister, her brothers. She often told me they were waiting for her. I could see her looking forward to them; she seemed peaceful when she did that. I know we all can't really explain what the other side is, but I do know, without a doubt, her angels were waiting for her, and she was well aware of that. I took comfort in that, and I knew she would be well taken care of. Thank you, Grace, just thank you. I remember telling the hospital staff that I would have switched places with her if I could have. She was my every-thing, and with her leaving my life would forever be altered. She cried a lot but only around me, as she didn't want the family to see her upset. One day she told me she was sorry she ruined my life because she felt I had made so many life choices based on her and her grandchildren. I made it clear to her that all my choices were exactly that: my choices. Everything I did was out of love. Again, the love that she showed me and the love I felt from her has always guided my life. I only remember breaking down once during that time. It was in Ben's arms. He was by my side and did the best he could with the situation. Somehow I kept it all together, picking up kids from school, homework, making sure everyone was fed, while still working to ensure I still had a paycheck coming in. She shared so much with me during those days, many things I haven't shared with anyone, and I probably never will. Because of those conversations, I was able to see my mother as a woman, as a human being. Someone who had dreams and loves. She was asleep during her very last days… Our conversations came to an end.

My conversations, then, turned heavily to God, to spirit. "Please take my mother in peace and with no pain. Help me get through this. Give me strength because I don't think I will be able to live through this." I just wanted peace for her, finally. I would return to faith heavily, although I had never really left it. The time came when her breath would start slowing down… I stayed all night with her the night before she passed. I was alone with her again. She never woke up, but I knew she would be leaving for good. As I sat in that chair, it dawned on me that I had experienced so many things in life to that point by myself, and I acknowledged my true strength that day. Watching my mother slowly leave my life was the hardest thing I have had to endure. I went back and forth with my emotions. When you love someone so much, you don't want them to leave, even if it means giving them peace. I know that sounds selfish, but it's exactly how I felt. I wanted to just lie down in the bed with her, hug my mother one last time. It was such a long time since she had been just my mother, meaning with becoming a grandmother at a young age, I had had to share her. I owed her my life, and selfishly I wanted some time alone with her back. Our alone time would be in peaceful silence. I prayed a lot and visualized a serene journey for her. I knew the angels would guide her home. I wasn't by her side when she took her last breath. My family wanted me to go home to try and get a little sleep since I had been up all night. I was home only for a few hours when my family arrived at my apartment to tell me she was gone. March 31, 2008: gone, the woman who gave me life, my hero, gone. My very first love, gone. My only trusted confidante in life was gone. *Gone.*

There we all were, my niece, my nephews, my aunt, and my cousin. I don't even remember who exactly told me that she was gone. I barely reacted. I immediately called work to tell them. That's when everything in my life went on cruise control, and nothing mattered. I had lost a great love in my life. My insides were numb. I don't specifically remember having any feelings. I often wondered how I would go forward without her. I knew at the end of the day that I didn't care what anyone else thought, and their opinions in life didn't matter to me. She was my everything and now she was gone. *Gone.*

I had to start to pave a new path on my own, and I had so many questions. Was I ready for that? Would I know what I was doing? Who would I run my ideas by now? I had built my adult life around my mother, and now a major piece was missing from my puzzle. I kinda predicted life would become a shitstorm for me after that, and there would be no one to really help me through it: everyone was grieving in their own way. In all honesty, what did *helping me through it* mean anyway? Change is always a guarantee in life, and I know most of us don't get a heads-up when something major is going to happen; I just know that the changes usually occur after the events you're hit with. I eventually was able to force out a smile, no matter what I was really feeling. It was easier for me just to put on a front because I just wanted everyone in my life to leave me alone. I didn't need anyone's tips on how to keep going. I knew I would find my path independently, exactly how I had always done. My mother would have known that; no one else did. Every single day was a struggle. Things that I liked to do didn't interest me anymore. Was it because I had shared some of those interests with my mom? I didn't care about watching figure skating because I did that with my mom. I stopped cooking certain dishes because they were her favorites—my meat loaf and my baked ziti. This would be a life-altering event for me, I was well aware of that. It would be easy to just say I was depressed. It was much more: a completely broken heart is beyond depression. Nothing was the same. But I guess I should never have expected things to be the same again. Hope, love, and peace—those came back with time. That doesn't mean that I don't miss her; it just means that I glued some of myself back together, even though there were now permanent cracks in my foundation.

I guess I'm just glad some form of myself remained: I was fine with all the changes that occurred. New hobbies, new interests helped get me past the day-to-day. Ben and I learned how to make soap. I was experimenting with new cooking recipes weekly and learning from different cultures. And my music, oh my music… It saved me from some dark days. I had playlists galore from Adele to Diana Ross to Ricky Martin. I knew the things I loved from my soul would always be my go-to. The music, the dancing, and the cooking would help me see the light again. I've always heard that even in your darkest moments there will always be a crack of light that penetrates. Even with that, it's all a choice, and I chose to come back into the light. I knew I wanted my real smile back, my light back. The smile that could light up a room. That smile my mother loved. I not only had to do this for myself, but I also had to do it for my mother. I wasn't ready to throw away a lifetime because I was only thirty-three when she passed. And yet again, I pulled all the strength I had inside me, got off the floor, and made the conscious choice to turn the page.

Her passing was twelve years ago now, and a lot has happened during that time. Her death taught me the lesson of always believing in love again and to keep going.

CHAPTER FIVE

Now I Need a Heart Monitor

Since the twenties is always a complex decade in life, any relationship starting out at that time can have its challenges. Ben and I were both not our complete selves to begin with. He was scared of any kind of true commitment, and I was trying to be something I wasn't to make it all work out. There was genuine love between us, but what everyone needs to understand is sometimes love just isn't enough. At least it wasn't enough to make that relationship work. The distance started by us spending more time apart. I was starting to concentrate on myself, and Ben would get lost in his world. Our world didn't seem to even exist at times, yet when we embraced, the love was still there. It was so complex and confusing. It wasn't intentional, it just happened, and I felt him drifting away even more than in just a physical sense. I even had the courage to tell him so.

"You are getting closer to me, and you don't like it" I mustered out right after breakfast one Saturday morning. He just stared at me with a blank look. Blank as a clean chalkboard. I made the decision to continue; I remember feeling like a few things had to be said.

"Your nephew came to visit, and we were all comfortable with each other, you liked it, and I could tell you were happy. That scared the shit out of you because that picture didn't match the one in your head, the one of you not having your family around or knowing about us!" This all made it too real for him, and he didn't like it.

He had a grin like he knew the truth had just been spoken. "Oh, Jenny, stop it." He responded, then hugged me. Nothing. Else. Said. And slowly he began to shut down even more.

He began to become something he didn't want to become, and I began to start to actually use my voice completely for the first time in my life. We weren't the same Benny and Jenny anymore. He hated that I called him that at times, yet he would refer to himself as Benny but only with me; I started to call him that after he took it upon himself to start calling me Jenny. Jenny was reserved for family and special people; he used it before he became special to me. It's hard to be on a different page when you really care about each other. I think that's part of the reason we stood together for so long. We grew up together, our twenties, then into our thirties. So much life happened during those decades. I knew things would start changing when I started to grow. When life started slapping me in the face with those life lessons we will all go through, I knew I wanted more. He walked away, we didn't discuss it, we both knew it would happen, and it did. Before Ben left, I had started to reinvent my body, my soul, my spirit, and I knew my relationship would be impacted, too. He didn't seem to like that I was finding some strength again.

In an odd way, he didn't want me to lean on him, but he also wanted me to lean on him one hundred percent. There is a duality in everything, and I mean everything. I think a lot of what he assumed I wanted in our relationship was what he concocted in his mind rather than just asking me about what I wanted. He thought I just wanted to be married, and honestly, I only wanted to be with him, in whatever way that meant. To seriously commit to being there for one another, that is what I had wanted. Our relationship came to an end after fifteen years right before the start of our forties.

I was very confused as to what to do when all this happened. There was a lot of crying and soul-searching for sure. There was a yoga retreat I had dreamed of going to for years; I decided to go, and oh boy, did I find my voice! I had a lot to say. I realized there that my voice had been swallowed a long time ago. I was a person I wasn't sure that I knew. And I have no one to blame for that but myself. I knew the time had come to work on that. I willingly let my voice be silenced because I was overwhelmed by life, and I was consistently doing what everyone around me told me to do. It was all their definition of the *right* thing, what I was *supposed* to do... Last time I checked, it was my life, so why was I living it according to everyone else's rules? Time had come to break through the restrictions of my family, the restrictions of my culture, and the restrictions of society!

Four days...it took four days, silent meals, daily yoga, meditation, journaling, crying, laughing, walking, hiking, and completely disconnecting from everything and everyone in my life to discover my true self. The transformation had started, and I could feel a shift all around me. I knew that I had started a new journey, a new chapter instantly. I loved Ben, but I loved me more, I had to begin to let him go. Kripalu had awakened every ounce of my being. I decided I was going to have a conversation with Ben in order to fully release him and move along with my life. It was a rainy Friday night, I was on the bus back from Massachusetts, and life felt ready for me. The bus ride was peaceful, and I had journaled a lot. I felt peace in my heart. Even the subway ride back to Brooklyn was a quiet moment for me—yes, the subway was quiet for me.

My cell was ringing nonstop as I was walking the few blocks from the subway to my apartment. I had just gotten the door open when a few texts came through simultaneously.

It was Ben.

We hadn't spoken in six months, completely no contact. He didn't know I had been away. My yoga calmness was still with me, but I slowly started think…

Jenny, are you home? the text read. *Hello?* said the next.

I took a deep breath and responded *Yes, I'm home.* I put down the phone and shook my head in disbelief.

Can I come over? The text that made me promptly sit down on the couch. I remember saying to myself *You're a big girl, Jenn. You can tell him what you need to… Remember you went fucking hiking in Massachusetts, and you don't fucking hike… You got this!*

Sure, when? I wrote and then gasped when I saw *RIGHT NOW!* You must be thinking Oh shit! Because I was…

My bag was still in the hallway! I decided I needed to jump right into this new chapter. Like deep dive right into it. "Okay," I said out loud, and then I ran to put my bag away and scope out the apartment really fast. I didn't care that he had lived there with me and knew where everything was; I wanted to make things a little more complicated and not that easy anymore when it came to me. Why should he think that time had stood still while he took a fucking siesta? Yes, I was still in my zen mode… Yogis can curse, ya know. It has nothing to do with anger, it's just the passion inside me. The bell rang, and my heart was beating faster. I unlocked the door, and there he stood smiling like everything was the same. I sat down on one end of the couch, the end I had always sat on. He was still smiling, but he seemed nervous. His whole vibe was anxious. I don't think I had ever seen Ben that way during the entire time I had known him, so that was interesting to me.

He nonchalantly said "What's going on?" I chuckled and replied "Not much," with a smile.

I remember thinking what the hell did he think was going on? It was a rainy Friday night, and we hadn't seen each other in months. Why not get to the point and tell me what the fuck he was doing here? But no, I couldn't say it like that because then I would sound like a bitch. So I just took a minute. My mind raced; what the hell was going on with him? I wanted to be back in my zen place and not where I was. At that point, he was pacing in front of the television…back and forth, back and forth while taking in short glimpses of me. I could tell he looked at what I was wearing: yoga pants, a namaste shirt, and a black cardigan. My yoga mat was in the new bag I had brought for the trip and was near the wall on the side of the television. A black bag with the seven chakra symbols all in bright colors.

He sat down on the other end of the couch and took a look at the bag. "Did you join a cult or something, Jenny?" he said looking confused.

I laughed. "No. So what have you been up to?"

He got up and started the pacing again when he blurted out "Look… I miss you, and I have never missed anyone in my life before, not even my parents!" He looked surprised at what had came out of his mouth. He continued. "I have never felt this way before. It's really bad. I don't know what to do. I can't stop thinking about you." He was frantic.

Wow! This man had walked away from our relationship and walked into the life that he had always said he wanted, so why was this happening? I was stunned, and all I could manage was "Okay, I miss you."

Once I said those words, Ben started to pace differently. He looked like he wanted to pace right on out of there. Wait, I know… I'll say it for everyone: *What the fuck?* Yep, everything and *nothing* had changed. Even the horrible feelings he was having couldn't get him to just believe in love and fall into it. He was scared. Bottom line. And so, the sunken feeling I had known all too well returned in an instant. He shut down again.

He stayed on the couch that night because it was too late for an hour drive back to the room he was renting, and the roads were a mess because of the rainstorm. Clearly two storms hit Brooklyn that night. Another reality check stormed right through the home we had built together. Ben and I saw each other a handful of times after that night—we still had so much unfinished business. Some was never reconciled, and I just had to let it all go to the wind when I released my old self. When I learned that I could not save Ben anymore and that it wasn't my job to save him, that's exactly when the new me had arrived. I was going to start saving myself and making myself number one for the first time. It has been years since I sent the last piece of communication to him. It simply stated "I have no bad feelings toward you, and I hope that you are doing okay."

I meant it. Every. Single. Word.

CHAPTER SIX

What's Going On with Jenn?

People in my life have all been asking the same thing for years: What's going on with Jenn? Then, the note-comparing among them begins. What's the bottom line of it all? Jenny is not giving them the attention she used to and so that means that something must be going on. We are all here on this earth to follow our own journey. That truly and undoubtedly means your journey, not your family's, friends', lover's, children's, employer's, and so on. You know the list goes on and on. You see, what everyone forgets is that those people are on their own journey, too. We as humans just forget because all those journeys are indeed embedded in one another. So we tend to pay more attention to those journeys and try to somehow fix them because reflecting on our own would take too much courage. My thoughts: be mindful of the easy buttons in life because those run out eventually, and all you're left with are the really hard buttons. And I'll be the first to admit that's no fun at all. The hard lessons of life always find us. Love is never an easy thing. The loss of it can knock you on your ass for quite some time.

Once again, my heart was completely shattered. Devastated is a close second in the lineup of emotions. This heartbreak stung deeper and longer. At times, I couldn't see my way past it. And this time the important person I would lean on was gone. I wanted to quickly get involved in anything but my everyday life. Getting back to the question at hand, *what's going on with Jenn?*, at this point in my life, I have earned the complete right to say it doesn't fucking matter, and frankly how dare anyone even raise that question when many folks have gone into some crazy stuff willingly and I just say "As long as you're happy"? I knew I had started a new chapter, and no one was going to tell me what was going to happen in it, not this time! Since I always have believed that my body is my temple, I rightfully started there. I was not the unhealthy person I used to be, and I wanted to take all of that to a new level for myself. Ask anyone who knows me: I never was one to get up and want to go work out. Boy, can things change in a moment!

That's when I started to actually like moving my body, and it felt good. There wasn't any *Oh, I gotta go work out. What a pain in the ass!* anymore. It just became a natural part of my life. It all clicked when I realized I had a close tribe of friends around me that are like-minded and really want to see a difference in the world. They all bring joy to my life and are the ones who inspired me to dream big. One by one, each of them had a special gift to share with me. They all taught me how to love my body and love myself. It's no wonder that each personal motivator I had taught me to raise my bar each time. What I had started on my own while hiking in Massachusetts expanded and brought me to meet new people every place I went. From yoga to Pilates to cycling, I tried my best to show up for myself and for those folks who led me to my true whole self. When I set out to find myself, I hadn't realized how lost I was. It came to a point where I questioned if the likes I had in life were really mine or not.

Keep in mind, not one of my tribe members knew how broken I was. On the outside, I looked like I had it together, and in many ways

I did. However, the insecurities of my childhood and teenage years would always surface no matter what. That voice telling me I'm still not good enough, still not thin enough, still not pretty enough. The same tune was there well into the middle of my forties. Plus, with the lost relationships in my past, the doubts came back strong. It's so easy for everyone to tell me "You're so beautiful"; what they all didn't understand was that I needed to feel it, or that negative voice would be there for the rest of my life. That voice is gone now, and the funny thing is, it left kinda overnight, which is hysterical after having it around for so long. What happened? you may be wondering. I felt in my gut that my mom was upset that I was being so bad to myself. Being hard on myself was always easy for me. I could beat myself up better than anyone. One day I heard my mom in my soul, and she said "Stop the nonsense already. Leave yourself alone." I didn't need to hear anything else: I knew she was pissed after all this time, so I knew I was done. You have to put your oxygen mask on first before you can help anyone else. We hear that all the time; however, I was finally taking action. It's all about me, and that's all that matters. Walking and yoga became a part of my daily life. I started to think more clearly, and my sleep improved. All the lights of wellness came on fairly quickly for me. I felt and looked younger. I was writing again, I was dancing again, life was flowing for me. When I would think about love, I would just think about me, and it was so refreshing.

That was an important stepping stone for my mind and then spirit healing which would follow. My forties began on a clean note. I was more myself than ever before. I had to believe in myself, and I had the love of a tribe behind me, too! You'll know your tribe when you see them, and sometimes if you're lucky enough, you'll be blessed to have a personal Jesus in there, too. Now, don't get me wrong: I'm spiritual but not super religious. I believe in God and Jesus. So don't get all worked up with me using that name. Understand that it's a source of strength and love. And when someone comes into your life like that, you'll know they are special and so is the relationship. To have someone befriend you when you are at your most vulnerable state, they don't know you, you're literally crying because life has been way too intense for a long period of time—yet, they look past the surface of your tears and just ask what they can do to help. That's when you know you're connected on a different level, a soul level. Spirit animals connected by the universe. You'll know it when you see it. It's just love.

It all wasn't overnight, but when the light came through I started to turn the page of love again, too. I knew I deserved love, and someone special would deserve my love. I didn't look at my past with scorned eyes, I looked at it with clear eyes and a wider heart. When I look at my tribe of phenomenal people with so much love in their hearts, I know that I owe them so much because they are the ones who put me back together each time I was torn apart by life's whirlwinds. I became stronger physically and spiritually, and my heart was filled up again. Keep in touch with your tribe: mine have always had my back. I love them all, and my life has been so enriched because of each and every one of them.

CHAPTER SEVEN

Finding My Love

Love is universal. I think we all forget that, or some just don't realize it. There are also those who don't want to acknowledge it. I think that happens out of fear. A universal love means we love everyone including their differences, and that is what scares people. *Fear* is a four-letter word just like *love*. So when love comes in and out of our lives, we either bask in the joy of it or we run the other way in fear. All that really exists in life is love, empathy, and peace, and those things can't be replaced. True success in life is knowing that kind of love. At the end of the day, we all want to know that we have led a great life, so stop looking at the material things around you. It doesn't matter how large your house is, how shiny your new car is, all of that doesn't speak to success at all. All those things may have taught you how to navigate money but not how to navigate life. There is a huge difference. This is where some overachievers get it wrong. The high grades, the awards, being number one, with all that you haven't really achieved success. It may have taught you discipline, structure, all good skills to have. Strip it all away, be in complete silence, and let go. This will allow the path of true love, peace, and empathy to begin to manifest in you. Joy is right at your fingertips.

Someone called me an overachiever a few months ago, and I laughed so hard about it. One would think my barely scraping by in high school and doing the same in my college years would never have classified me as an overachiever. However, then the clarification came: I'm an overachiever in life. Wow! That blew my mind because I realized it was true. I have challenged myself in life without needing a push from anyone, not even my mother. I raise my bar all by myself, and I do the best I can to reach it. That's why I knew I had raised the bar when it came to love in my life again. Roger entered my life when I wasn't sure I would find true love. I believe it existed; I just hadn't felt it in my core before. I was so nervous to meet him in person after weeks of chatting about everything we could think of. I still smile at the thought of the first text messages we exchanged.

Hi, Jenn! Can you help me with something? When you take a shower, don't you wash your hair first? Or am I crazy?

I laughed, then responded *I would say yes, I wash my hair first. Do you have a debate going on about that? (wink emoji)*

It turned out his youngest son was getting ready for bed slowly, and Roger was trying to get him moving along… And with that he had me laughing the rest of the evening. I had enjoyed myself so much, it had been a long time since I felt that way—and I mean genuinely—I stayed up past my curfew, which Roger would love to remind me of and took pleasure in helping me break it all the time… I knew we had something unique, the fear of being hurt again was so strong as always, but I knew I had to jump right in. He told me I was beautiful inside and out, it was genuine, it was honest. I could see it in his eyes. No one had ever told me that I was beautiful with their eyes. It was so special.

From the evening of our first date, there was no pretending we were something else. You know what we all do: put on this front so we're not as vulnerable. Then the relationship starts on some level of falsehoods. We didn't do that; it all came naturally and organically. We had so much in common, yet led very different lives. He answered some key questions for me, and he surprised himself with some of his responses.

"Would you ever get married again?" I asked as he took a sip of his old-fashioned. "Yes!" he replied with no hesitation. His slight grin was already growing on me.

I thought, *Okay...that seemed genuine.* I could tell he believed in love, don't ask me specifically why, I could just tell; my inner soul knew it.

"Okay, next important question," I said with a shy grin.

He smiled. "Uh-oh."

"I've been easy with you all night, and we aren't getting any younger." I looked him directly in his eyes quite seriously and intensely. "Would you have more children?" I didn't hesitate, not one little bit. My eyes were locked in his.

Without the blink of an eye.

Roger quickly responded, "I know what my answer should be at my age, but I know what my heart says the answer is, and it's yes, I would. A woman growing life inside her is the sexiest, too!" His face screamed *I can't believe I just said that,* but I could tell he also wanted to say what was true to his soul.

At that moment, I knew that we would embark on something special. I also knew I had to challenge myself and really think about the Having a Child question I had asked him. It was something I had always wanted in my life. Yet, I had a weird feeling when I heard his answer. I knew I had some personal exploring to do. Roger was a gentleman, he was kind; yet, he had sass to him, which I needed. I'm a Leo born in August, from a Latin family of strong women, so damn straight, I needed someone who could handle me and not be afraid of all of it. He was a Leo, too, and it was like the fire of the two lions had been ignited! The intensity of our relationship would have caused the average person to run in fear because it was a lot. Not us—we loved every moment. What used to be insecurities for me were gone. And for him, I showed him genuine true love that he hadn't had before. I loved him for him and all that came with it. I respected him and he respected me. It was my first time being involved with someone who had children. The love of his children was evident from the moment we first spoke. I could physically feel his love for his children when he spoke about them. I fell in love with his heart. I knew his children meant the world to him. The sign of a really good man is how he loves and cares for his children. For me, that means even when a marriage separates and ends, the relationship with one's children should still be a priority, and it was for Roger. I loved him for that. I loved him for bringing me back to life and finding true love with him. True love asks for nothing: all we needed was each other. The world felt safer when I was in his arms. I could exhale and relax every time he hugged me. We could easily call each other telepathically. That started to happen immediately. I knew he would be the man I would spend the rest of my days with, because when you spend endless hours, endless days together just talking and being with one another, nothing else matters. We didn't need to see the next movie coming out or any other superficial thing. We were enough for each other.

CHAPTER EIGHT

When Bad Things Happen...Again

I have definitely been blessed with true genuine love in my life. I could feel that from a very young age. The love of my mother, the love of my family, my grandmother, aunts, uncles, cousins, nieces, and nephews. And I can't forget the special loves that have crossed my path and enriched my life, too. I'm so grateful to have experienced love in so many ways. It's a beautiful feeling.

When Roger and I met, things were spinning fairly quickly for both of us. We had such different life stories but seemed so alike. Right from the start, we knew we had a very special connection. It didn't take many dates to realize that. We took a leap of faith with each other, tested new waters. He was a little older than me, and he had three children. That was all uncharted territory for me, yet it felt exactly right. I was a younger, Latin gal from Brooklyn with a sass he had never experienced before; he felt at home with me. Our relationship was beautiful, we respected one another, we were important to each other. We could communicate with our eyes. I could sense when he was thinking about me. This was all scary to both of us; yet, we knew it was so meant to be. We were emotionally honest with each other from the beginning. Neither of us wanted to get hurt again. Our hearts wouldn't have been able to take another hit. So we kept our feelings open and our communication solid. From our very first kiss, he told me there would soon be anarchy between us. We both knew that meant something like chaotic passion between two people in an amazing way. We had an intense connection, there was a definite magnetic chemistry between us.

"Roger, let me ask you a question." I had a smirk on my face because I wanted to hear his response. "Which do you think is stronger, a lion or a lioness?" I slyly asked and raised one eyebrow as I stared at him.

He responded fairly quickly. "Well, the lion, of course! Silly girl!"

I smiled, and before I could respond he added, "Did I just give the wrong answer and now you'll never let me take you out again?"

I laughed. "There isn't a right or wrong answer, so I guess you got lucky…"

"Then, why ask the question, Jenn?" he said, grazing his chin with his right index finger.

"I just wanted to hear your response," I said as I leaned in a little closer.

"Why does my response matter?" He looked puzzled and excited at the same time.

"Who said that it did? It's just a question. Don't take it so seriously." I winked to close the topic down.

"I must say, I am absolutely intrigued by you, Jennifer." Roger smiled.

From that moment on he knew he was dealing with a woman with a fascinating mind, and he was on board one hundred percent!

We had a whirlwind love affair, and we fell in love very quickly. I cared about this man with all my heart. He was romantic, sweet, kind, generous, funny, and he had a special flair to him. He would sport a fedora just for the hell of it and didn't care who didn't like it. His style was clean-cut, and he always looked relaxed. He was tall with dark hair and deep brown intense eyes, overall a distinguished Humphrey Bogart type. We loved listening to music together. We both liked all kinds of music, but we connected the most over R&B. It spoke to both our souls. We loved eating out and trying new restaurants. Roger caught on very quickly that I loved steak. I'm a very healthy eater, but when I go out, I like a good steak. He made sure to take me to the places where I'd be happy, and he was amazed that I was always worried about menu prices.

"Where do you want to go tonight?" Roger asked one evening while he was wrapping up work.

"I wanted to try this restaurant not too far from where I live, but I looked at the menu and it's kind of pricey. I think I'm going to look up some other places before you get here." I meant every word because I was never the type to just want to spend people's money.

"Wow, you are amazing—you are actually concerned about how much I would spend on dinner later. No date has ever said that to me before. You constantly surprise me, Jenn."

The time would fly when we were together. We could talk for hours about everything. We loved each other unconditionally and accepted one another for who we were; we never put on an act with each other. We were our natural selves. He was a godsend in my life. I knew instantly that our souls were connected. He made me feel special, and he loved me so deeply. I always felt his love, and that was the first time I experienced that. We wanted to spend the rest of our lives together, but time wasn't on our side. To put it all in one simple state-ment…I met the love of my life and he died ten months later.

The one thing I immediately said to myself was *Oh, okay, I guess life is giving me another sharp lesson here…* I was in shock once again. This time it was surreal. The shock of finding love and losing love so quickly is beyond measurable. I didn't want to think about what lesson this could be. I only knew I was down on the ground once more. I have no words to express how hard it is to watch someone you love die and to then experience it again: it is earth-shattering. I lost my love, I lost myself, I lost our future. It was all gone in the blink of an eye. Cancer quickly took Roger, from routine surgery to finding a growth outside his pancreas. I still haven't made complete sense of all of it. The details don't matter, someone else I deeply loved was taken from me. I realize now more than ever that it really doesn't matter what someone dies of or how old they were, when someone you love passes, it shakes you to the core with pain. It's so common to ask how did someone die when death is mentioned. I'm just not really sure why, as a society, we think that matters. It seems like an automatic question for many. If I had a dollar for every single time someone asked me what my mother died of or what Roger died of, I would have a significant amount of savings, and I mean significant. And with my humor, there have been many times that I wanted to make something up, like a crazy story not involving anything having to due with illness. It's not to make light of their passing; it just gets exhausting explaining something in detail. There really is no point to it.

I miss hearing his voice, I miss his hugs and his arms around me, I miss his love. I never asked God or the universe *Why did this happen? Who was I to ask that?* I already had learned not to ask that because you'll never get an answer, so don't torment yourself. This time I felt like I had left my own body. I was just trying to hold on, hold on to life and hope once again. This went even deeper this time for me. I had lost the love of my life: it wasn't the ending of a relationship, he didn't choose to leave. The connection was still there, he just wasn't physically there anymore. The pain was intense, and there is no way to measure it, a pain that I wouldn't wish upon anyone, even the most evil person. I could barely tell people. I would break down each time. I could hear the shock in their voices, not knowing what to say. Everyone giving light suggestions on how to keep going, that I'm still young and don't let this ruin me. Of course, I realized all of this on my own. It's just… How do you start to think about the future when you still belong to someone else in soul and spirit? Whatever dreams we discussed would never happen. How do you do an immediate rewrite of what would have been your next chapter?

Days can be a struggle at times, keeping myself in the light. The light means different things to different people. To me it meant continuing to live my life and doing the things I loved. I don't waste time anymore. I try to level up each and every day. I do that for him; I do that for myself; I do that for our love. I don't ask myself why cancer took two people I adored because it won't bring them back, either.

I felt Roger's spirit around me very quickly. I knew the feeling well because my mother had been around me for the last dozen years. Now the feeling was just more intense. Spirit has helped keep me going. I'm sure it's hard for some of you to understand, and I get it. You won't be able to understand unless you've had the experience. What gives me comfort is knowing their genuine true love for me continues on; I still feel it. I thank him every single day for coming into my life. For loving me. For sharing his life, his memories, his heart with me. Love is a crazy, crazy thing. You never know how or when it will come along. It's always a big unknown, but we all seek it and rightfully so. Love is a beautiful thing. It's amazing and painful at the same time. Love brings so many different things into our lives. I know we had something special when I not only fell in love with the man, I fell in love with the father he was, the human being he was. Our spirit will forever be intertwined, for our love will never die.

CHAPTER NINE

Leo, Transformation, and Full Reimagination

Roger passed, and I didn't think I would be on the page that I was on, but there I was. Since I had always had pets in my life, I started to think about maybe getting one again. My allergies seemed to be in a good space after I moved away from Brooklyn. I thought maybe I could do this again. I made the decision to bring a dog into my life. I had been a cat mom before—both Sebastian and Max had brought such happiness into my life—but I wanted something different now.

Leo became a huge ray of sunshine in my life from the moment I laid eyes upon him. He provided me so much love even before he came home. There have been many times in my life where I knew that person, animal, thing would help me turn a page. It's more than just saying it, it was hope, it goes much deeper. I named my sweet little puppy Leo Luna Alemany. There is always meaning behind everything in my life. Luna was my mother's maiden name. To me it signifies so much strength, so much love, it's important to me. The Alemany is very obvious. It signifies my Cuban roots; it's part of me, it always has been. It didn't surprise me that my little Leo is a

Havanese: he has Cuban roots, too! No matter the circumstances, never forget what you are made of, where you came from, and where you have been. Leo, that name has so much meaning behind it. I'm a Leo born smack in the middle of August. My beautiful grandmother was a Leo, and she started my entire family. One of my aunts is a Leo, and a strong, badass woman for sure. One of my closest cousins is also a Leo: she's a rock-star warrior without a doubt. I also have younger little Leos that have also entered my life recently, too. I can sense their strong spirits as well. My love was also a Leo. He was a strong lion and an amazing spirit. His roar of life took me into a great adventure from the moment of our first exchange. I hold the name Leo close to my heart. I now have a Leo-symbol tattoo on my foot also. When I decided on naming my sweet baby puppy Leo, it all made exact sense, and it was meant to be. There was no doubt in my heart that his name should be something important to me. And it all came together exactly as it should be. His spirit is strong, and he's sassy, too. It all makes sense because all the Leos in my life, including myself, we have the strength of lions and lionesses. So every time I call Leo or hug him, it's me giving love to all my loves and myself.

I watched my mother and my love, Roger, pass on very quickly. So you see, life forced me to transform. I wasn't really given a choice; however, I decided to accept the transformation and not resist it. Both of them leaving my life shocked me into reality. Their deaths took my heart and viciously tore it apart. You kinda have to become a new version of yourself because the old one is gone anyway. Resistance would not have done a damn thing for me. It wouldn't have brought back the two people who had genuinely loved me unconditionally, the only two people who had my complete trust because they earned it. Two phenomenal human beings who I was blessed to have had in my life. So I turned the pages again, and again. I kinda lost track of which transformation I'm on because so many things have happened, and they were all mini evolutions, too. Let's say we are on Jenny 4.0 now!

I wouldn't be the person I am today if I did not have the love and the loss that I have experienced. The funny thing is…my heart is still full. The cracks are still there, yet it is fuller than it has ever been. I know with each loss, I have learned to love even more deeply. That may sound crazy, but it is so true. The losses have opened my eyes to all the life that is around me. And don't get me wrong, my eyes have always been open, they are just looking at everything with a clearer lens. With each pain I have felt, it forced me to dive deeper into life. I felt kinda like I had no other choice. I knew I was not meant to drown but to fly. I didn't see any other path. It is like the pain filled my life and made me become more of my true self. Not the self that would make everyone else around me happier. For once in my life, I had to close everyone around me down in order to put myself in the driver's seat of my own life. I knew I cared too much for others, and I wouldn't be able to not help with all things, so I had to shut down shop in a sense. I knew in my heart that the only way back to me was to put blinders on so I would be able to only see myself. I knew that the time had come to change the course of my life. Honestly, what did I have to lose? After decades of worrying about others, I had to worry about myself and only myself. The guilt that would naturally come with being selfish is a hard thing. Not everyone has that guilt, but when you do, it is strong. So like everything else, I prayed and meditated on it, and spirit gave me the answer. It was now my time!

After a deep dive across the board of my life and deeper into spirituality, I knew that having a life with pure joy was going to be my next chapter, that life would get easier because I had lifted all the boulders off my back. That doesn't mean that I don't have semihard days; it just means that I get up and dust myself off faster than ever before. I now listen to the trees, the wind, the birds. I listen to the life around me. I take things slowly. I absorb the beauty of life in all forms. It's because I know it could all be gone in a moment's notice. When people that you love pass on, many folks acknowledge it, and it gives them some food for thought in their own lives, but often enough we easily get back into the grind and close our eyes again to the beauty of life. I say that because I did that after my mom passed, but after life pushed me into the deep end of the pool again, I had to say *No fucking way...* I'm not staying down this time. Give it all to me, test me in every which way...I refuse to give up. And not only do I refuse to give up, I will raise my vibration of kindness, of love, and of hope more and more with each passing day. I believe that when you are in your greatest pain, that is when you realize your full potential and what you really have to give in this life. For me, it was after all my pain that I knew that I had a voice and I knew I needed to share that voice with others. Share it with all the women out there and share it with my Latinx community.

To my core, to my soul there are certain traits of mine that are within me and always will be. I can be stubborn at times, yet that has lightened up. I could want things really fast; now I take a moment to pause and not seek immediate satisfaction. I've realized in my maturity that sometimes the best things in life are worth waiting for. I have a small notebook of thoughts, simple statements I've passed along to others on my journey. Here's number 15: *Sometimes quick satisfaction may not be the best long-term. Have patience, sometimes waiting, then getting something could end up being the best ride of your life.* I now apply that to everything across the board. Don't cheat yourself. Life is too short. I try to apply light and love to everything these days. Let me set the record straight: it's not easy at all! Especially when you are giving love to those who may have done wrong by you. Forgiveness...that's a whole other chapter. What I've learned is the grudge or anger you hold is just going to eat way at your insides. It kinda happened to me. Ulcers, severe long-term stomach issues, high blood pressure, and a host of other little health ailments. So you see, it's totally not worth it. Let it go. So those that may test you in their own special ways…I take a deep breath and wish them light, love, and clarity for their lives…and then turn the page. I apply this in everyday life as well, especially when I get worked up about small stuff. It's not worth the energy. That's when you kinda know the reimagination is starting. I do have to acknowledge that when I look back at my old self, I had way too much on my plate, and that was my plate of life collectively. So everyone who may have assumed that I was just a negative person in the past: No, I'm just someone who didn't want to burden others and ask for help. So I drowned myself with responsibilities and didn't come up for air.

Now I say No! I put myself first, and there is no question about it anymore. My mind, body, and soul thank me for finally learning that lesson. My health internally and physically have been improved immensely from the past. My diet was horrible, exercise was a dirty word to me, my body was toxic. It took a lot of sickness to pass through me for me to really wake up, but I did finally. At age forty-six, I walk three to five miles every day. I practice yoga. I meditate. I sleep eight hours a night, and I go to bed early to accomplish that. My food is clean and whole. My body is in the best condition it has ever been. I feel healthy, alive, and I love myself. I have more energy than ever before. It's a lot of hard work and discipline, but when you really start to enjoy feeling good, it's not work at all. It's just doing the best that you can for yourself. Notice the theme: *you, you, you*. And it's okay, everything will be okay. Everyone will live if you don't prioritize them. Life will go on. Put your heart into yourself. I give you permission. Do it for you. I had to, and it's fucking amazing!

The journey for discovering ultimate self-love had begun for me years ago, but I knew the final breakthrough was near. I think as people we have to do our darn best to get up and keep going. And that's the hard part, taking the first step. It's been more than a year since Roger's passing, and many things have happened in my life. I'm not the same woman I was a year ago, and yet I'm more of myself for the first time in my life. The way that I love and care for myself is of the utmost importance. I'm the leader of my life, and no one else is. We all stop ourselves from acting upon what feels right because of the rules and regulations we put on each other. Because of that realization…I stopped putting the so-called rules on myself. Every day I just listen to my body, and I do what it needs. If I walk, I walk. If I don't, then I don't beat myself up about it anymore. One day it just dawned on me, why was I so hard on myself about everything? I realized I had to let go of that, too, in order to fully move forward. I don't get on the scale anymore and concentrate on the number: I know how I feel. When I'm doing right by my body, I'm naturally lighter. I always do a yoga session for multiple reasons, and that session tells me way more important information than the scales ever provided.

CHAPTER TEN

Trees, Mother Earth, and the Universe

Have you ever just stared at a bunch of trees? For me, it helps to clear my head. Even if I start thinking about the trees too much, like *Look at the leaves on that one, look at that other one,* and so on. At the end of the day, you are just talking about the trees. It's all life, it's nature. It's beauty.

Whenever I meet someone who really needs to slow down and take a minute, I tell them to go stare at some trees. When you bring nature into your life, it invites a sense of calmness. If you are truly open to it, it can change your life, and the funny thing is it was always there, all around you. It gives you a minute to breathe. A minute to relax. A minute to realize that things can slow down and still be okay. If you are like my formal self…you feel great accomplishment in getting one thousand things done in a day, checking off all those things on your list, check, check, check. Those checklists never opened up my eyes to life, they just satisfied a momentary need for control and a guaranteed moment of satisfaction, check. I know now, the greater accomplishment is finding a new layer of myself that I didn't know existed before in one day. Crazy how things change.

I started appreciating nature more in my early twenties when I went to college. It was the first time I can remember really taking in my surroundings. Appreciating life, realizing that there was more outside of New York City. I began going outside to think and clear my head; it was a beautiful thing. I can't say I kept it up all the time because I know I didn't. Going back to the noise of the city completely silenced nature in any form for me. Let's say I found it again in my late thirties. The funny thing is when I found it again, I appreciated it so much more. I cherished life so much more. I was grateful for the breath I took. I was thankful that I had the opportunity to experience nature freely. Whenever I feel lost, I go for a walk. I find a tree or two, and I just clear my mind. I don't ask for answers. I just ask for clarity of mind, honesty of speech, and true love in my heart, for those are the things that will keep me on the right path. Everything else will fall into place, exactly as it's supposed to. I've learned to trust the timing of my life.

Shortly after Roger passed, I visited Kripalu again. While I was there, I thought about donating a tree to be planted in his name. I felt like I wanted life in some fashion to grow in his honor, and I wanted it to be known. I started to look into it, but my soul wasn't yearning to do it, I wanted more. You see, a tree at Kripalu could benefit many by being there, but what if I made myself the tree and allowed that to grow in his honor? I put all that I could into doing the right thing and helping others. If I helped myself grow the best I can, and the possibility of others growing from that too… Look at how amazing that could be. So, I planted the tree quite some time ago, no announcement needed. I'm a work in progress, but what I can say for sure is I've accelerated growth, so watch out! Look at the trees, listen to them rustle in the wind, observe how they change color, and how easily they let go. Something to think about when you look at life. What I did was I put the tree of my twentysomething self right next to newly self-planted tree, and I told them how beautiful they both were and are. I told them I wanted them to grow even more, and in order to do that they would have to shed all their leaves. Mother Earth would be blessing them both, so let the evolution begin. When we grow, we give ourselves the opportunity to become an elevated version of ourselves. And I don't know about most of you, but I know I'm really fucking amazing right now! However, to see myself even more balanced, more spiritual, to be at peace with life would be phenomenal. So I do my best to strive for more growth, more grounding. More of a connection with source. It's easy for most folks to list their favorite things and define that as who they are, but there is so much more to learn about oneself. When you strip all those things away, then you are left with the real you. Bare, down to your bones. Like the trees, bare.

Evolving with grace is a high spiritual practice that will quiet your soul, and you will feel peace. I feel evolving with grace is really accepting things for what they are and having gratitude toward everything. When I realized that I was experiencing this, I thanked everything in the universe because I knew it was a blessing to just realize that this was happening. I accept all the things that transpire in my life, and I also acknowledge I have made the choices to experience everything happening in my life. When you're able to be truly genuine with these revelations, then the quiet and peace will come. You stop pushing so hard on the things you have no control over. It's said so many times by everybody these days, but try to seriously put it into action. Life will then become easier. Mother Earth has been telling us these things all along. I've grown with all that I can think of. My frame of mind, how serious I am, my body, and how I care for it. My mind, body, and spirit connectivity is at its all-time best. I realized now twenty years later that all the stressors around me were out of my control, but I always had control over how I let them control me. At least I have learned that lesson now and didn't let another twenty years pass by. It's important to always keep learning, it keeps the mind growing. This will also enhance your sense of freedom.

If I didn't speak of freedom before, I should have. With each evolution of myself, my freedom also elevated. We are all technically free, but we don't all admit to the prison we keep inside ourselves. My freedom came to me little by little, but each time it was invigorating, and I loved it. That in itself is worth all the soul-searching, all the tears. Trust your evolution it's meant to be a part of your story. Your entire story is important, so be sure to cherish every minute of it. Life can sometimes be a merry-go-round, and sometimes it can definitely be a roller coaster; take a chance on both experiences, and life won't be the same. You have to let yourself try both. It's worth it. I guess when I think about it all, it's hard to say what would be the one thing I would say to my eighteen-year-old self. On one hand there is so much that I would say, and yet on the other hand I don't want to say anything at all. I feel like I would let the dice roll on my old self, let the choices be made, and let's see what would happen. I have a magnet on my fridge that reminds me every single day to learn from everything. And that includes the bad stuff. That is sometimes a hard pill to swallow, because then you are reminded of the difficult times, and who wants to relive that? I think for me I don't go through every single moment of the negative: I try my best to limit the amount of time I focus on it, make it an abbreviated session of quick analysis. Sometimes you just have to get in and out, dirty and fast.

When I look at that long-term relationship that ended, I no longer analyze it to figure out what was going on with Ben, or what was going on with me at the time for that matter. I actually thank him and the universe for putting it all into my life. I know that is a funny thing to say. How does someone thank someone else for heartbreak?

I had to learn to accept the entire package of that relationship. Every single moment that happened was exactly supposed to be. And don't get me wrong, that was a tough mountain to climb, and then throwing all the shit of the past down that mountain was even harder, but I did it. There were a lot of tears, laughing, and accepting my own actions in everything that transpired. That part happened organically, and I was thankful for that, too. I recently listened to the podcast *Super Soul Sunday* with Ali MacGraw. She spoke of past complicated loves, and I finally realized how poorly I had treated myself, and I don't mean in the obvious ways like fluctuating weight and sleeping more. I stayed around…I stayed around people who treated me poorly in their own ways. I openly and actively accepted their bad behavior. Thank you, Universe! Yes. I have to say that because it's true. It was just another lesson. One night after a bender drinking session, Ben came home, and he was agitated. It was because he wasn't feeling well. I was just trying to take care of him, and he didn't like it. I never judged him for his drinking. I could always see there was so much more behind it. He held a lot of sorrow and pain on the inside. He never told me that, I just knew. He didn't want my care that evening. For the first time, he told me he hated me. It stung through my entire core, my soul. I still remember the feeling, and I tear up when I think about it. He retracted the statement very quickly, telling me he didn't feel that way, hugging me while he said it. Nothing can take away the feeling of being told you are hated by the person you truly love. What I do know is Ben didn't hate me, he hated himself in that moment, and he could no longer contain it. I hit another level of freedom with this AHA moment. I was able to forgive myself and forgive him just a little more. I do hope his inside pain has healed or it's on the road to peace. That is what I truly wish for him. Now you see what I mean about layers of hidden things that need to be uncovered. I thought I had no more tears for Ben, but yet the universe showed me differently.

I was truly an altered being. I didn't question these things coming out because I was renewed every single time. I wouldn't say a better self—it was more of a complete grounding situation. A grounded person. It takes some getting used to the resets, but I gotta tell ya, they are totally worth it. I realize now the first reset started with my mother passing. I won't say that I'm still going through the process of looking at it. Her leaving my life catapulted it into what felt like was another complete hemisphere. I did a reset on so much at that point, I just didn't realize I was actively doing it. She gave me the push to want more and go get it, now. There was no more waiting. That's why I started moving things along and quickly at certain times. I was no longer wasting time. One thing in life is guaranteed: life is an unreliable narrator.

CHAPTER ELEVEN

Forgiveness and Rebirth

This writing adventure started in July of 2019, and it's still a well-kept secret at the moment. I really like that my first book will have a *Wow!* factor. I deserve a *Wow!* factor! Just sayin'. As I just wrote that, I realized my writing adventure officially started on June 6, 2017, to be specific. For as long as I can remember I have been writing, but never did I think of publishing anything, let alone a book. My health took priority in 2017. I decided to move away from the only life I had known that year, so I knew my endurance and stamina would be tested. I had come to the conclusion that I would never allow outside forces to impact my health again. The slew of health issues ranged from high blood pressure to gastric ulcers to chronic migraine headaches to name a few, and they all would be exacerbated by stress. Stress from work, stress from family, the list went on and on. Since we can't walk in one another's shoes… I often felt the folks around me didn't seem to take into account all that I was dealing with. You see, race comes into play here, too. As a Latina from a poor family, I was behind from the start, and people don't seem to get that. I knew things in my life had to change. I was going to make a difference for me and a difference for my community, someway, somehow. It was time to start to sharing my voice, my journey, and I wrote a short article about my health journey. That little story was about one human being empathetic to another and showing them hope again. It was published on June 6, 2017, and that day would have been my mother's seventy-fourth birthday. That was no coincidence—I believe there are no coincidences in life. I made the decision to speak my voice for the first time, which isn't easy for a private person like me. I knew that my voice had been silenced for too long, so I jumped right in.

On that day, my mother was telling me to go for it, people were going to listen. That day felt like I had just set sail on new voyage; it was exhilarating! I celebrated my mother's birthday for the first time in nine years because of that published story. Thank goodness that I kept so many mental notes from that year which evolved into this book. I remember multiple folks asking me "Are you a writer now?" I would gently giggle about that; however, somehow the universe pulled me in that exact direction, and it felt exactly right! I had found my purpose, and my mother has been confirming that message from beyond all along. When I was out and about running all kinds of errands that year preparing for my move, I would jot down ideas and thoughts because I was really noticing life again. Always paying attention to those around me would give me the words for my writings. I pay attention to what is being said between the lines, too. There is something about the words people use to say things, and I listen to all of it. Life and spirit were both speaking to me, and I could hear clearly.

It's also been a year since I began working with a life coach and a spiritual adviser. When the topic of forgiveness was mentioned to me, I didn't realize I had a layer to unfold there, too. The honest truth is I hadn't focused on or thought of many folks from my past in a very long time. I had put those chapters of my story away so many years ago that I wasn't sure where forgiveness would bring me. My coach sensed that my forgiveness of many was true and genuine. What she was referencing was something different. She asked me to light a candle and say a prayer for a few folks from my past. Holy shit! Would I be able to do this? Yes, now there is true genuine love in my heart for all human beings. But this was next level. In all my readings and my learnings over the past year, letting go of so much became easy once I started the process. Now it was time for me to wish well for those who have hurt me, deliberately or not. I had to tackle each person's prayer one slow step at a time because I had no idea that there would be an emotional upheaval inside myself along with this.

One by one, I forgave family, old lovers, and former friends. I cried, then I cried some more, and I genuinely wished them all love and light. I knew the pain they had inflicted on me was only because their own hearts had once been broken so severely, that they only knew pain. This cathartic ritual was the best advice I could have undertaken for myself. I was released from any anguish I was subconsciously holding on to. I think as humans, we all fail to understand that others are just trying to make it through life just like we are. I realized a rebirth of myself had transpired, and I had another huge boulder lifted off my back. These folks no longer impacted my life. They were truly in the past. I was free from so much; the liberation I felt was a feeling like no other. I knew things would work out for me no matter what. The definition of true love had found me, and I realized what my life was all about.

And then I became an unconditional lover of life, and everything immediately started flowing to me. The unconditional part truly meant the love of every ounce of every thing. If it rains, I don't wish for the sun. I thank the drops coming down around me for nourishing the earth and replenishing all. If it's a sunny day, I try not to get into how hot I feel —and that one is a hard one for me…I don't like it too hot. I really try to just be thankful for the sun because I may not see it on dark days. I'm grateful for the dark days, too, for I wouldn't appreciate the light as much! I was able to realize how easy it was to go down an avenue where everything seems dim. When life had put boulders on me, it was all super heavy and it was easy, simple to go to the dark. Now, I know how easy it is to put it all in the other light direction. The joy I finally felt in my soul was amazing. I would share some of this with some close loved ones but not many. When folks don't know true spirituality, it's hard for them to understand some things. I know it may sound crazy, but everything in life is not supposed to be seen and or be logical. There are so many unanswered things in life, and I trust that.

The things I believe in the most cannot be seen. Love, faith, and hope have seen me through my darkest hours when I felt so alone. Each time I was down on the ground, that is what got me up. *Clarity*, what can I say… We throw that word around these days, but the only true clarity that exists is being in true alignment with our own selves. Today, I came to the realization that those who I loved in a romantic way before didn't really have my true love as a whole because I didn't love myself. So I genuinely forgive those who hurt my heart because I wasn't giving them a whole person, and everyone deserves a whole person.

In time and in meditation, you fine-tune who you really are. Keep in mind we were all born as who we really are. We just begin altering that person as its true self with what we perceive is wanted by the people we interact with. I was in amazement when this all finally dawned on me. So every single relationship I have had up until this present moment was technically half-baked! Now, I like the Ben & Jerry's Half Baked ice cream, but I didn't want a life that was half-baked or half-anything for that matter.

If I could have told my younger self about this realization, I know I wouldn't have believed myself. After all the pain, I was realizing a whole lot, and it was invigorating, something along the lines of having a new life ready to live. It saddens me to see so many folks in my life go through true pain and continue to dwell in it without directly realizing it. Anniversaries and birthdays of my lost loved ones recur; however, I no longer cry on those days. I genuinely rejoice that they were present in my life and think about how honored I am to have had the opportunity to love them. The sad questioning of how, when, and why they left when they did is no longer present. They are happy that I'm truly living my life, and I mean truly. My life is not an automatic one: I open my eyes and thank spirit for waking me up with another blessed day each morning. I ask the universe to surround my days with light, love, and joy. I walk outside with my dog, and I thank mother earth for holding us in her arms. I wish the birds a good morning, and I take a deep breath. Nothing else matters. I stay on that frequency and vibration all day long! Sometimes the frequency rises even higher when I throw in a dance at some point in the day. It's just that simple… It took all those life lessons to really teach me that I control all of it. I always did. I'm truly free now in so many ways that I wasn't before.

A life without judgment is so important to one's self-growth. Don't judge yourself, and definitely don't judge others. In my rebirth, I no longer judge myself. See, we are truly all here for love, and that's what it will always go back to. And loving our differences is all part of it, so why is that so hard for everyone to understand? We do know we can never walk in each other's shoes; it's just not possible. We can do our best to empathize; however, it goes so much deeper than that. Sometimes, it's best just to say *I love you* and just be still, be silent. Cry if you need to cry with each other. Be mindful of the words you use during any life changes, transitions, rebirths, and such. Those words will be remembered because they will sting somehow, and you won't know why because we can't feel each other's true emotions. Rebirth. Just treat yourself and others like human beings. Act with love and kindness always.

CHAPTER TWELVE

Here We Are...
Spirit, Mashed Potatoes, and All

S o when you have a loved one who passes on, and you truly had a connection on earth, it will be around you universally: that connection doesn't die. Love doesn't die. This is why spirit doesn't believe in death. Right now, right here, we are all still truly together. Take the physicality out of all of it. We are just in our chosen human forms for now, and yes, I did use the word *chosen*. That's a whole other story down the road. Here are a few things I have observed.

As everyone maps out their life and exactly how they want it to be, what they don't do is shake that up and pick up the pieces, then rebuild from there. The mapping out is easy. The shake-up is the hard part, but no one will be willing to do that. So, we head out on the journey we mapped out, and then the curve balls come into play. Then the record playing the same old tunes happens to start playing all by itself. Then we make the same old statements. Why is this happening to me? Why do bad things happen to good people? What did I do to deserve this? Every time I want to start something new, there is always something stopping me. Reality check…*you are the one thing stopping yourself!* Not the universe, not the people around you, no one but you.

Now I know that is a hard pill to swallow, but if you decide to open up to it, life will start to get a lot easier. Take some true ownership of your destiny. We are all meant to serve a purpose on this earth. It's just so many of us get confused as to what our purpose is. It's not necessarily doing something you're good at or having the family you set out to have. I'm very good at a lot of things, but I know now none of those things are my true purpose. You see, I've taken just about forty-six years to analyze the events of my life and connect all those dots. And I'll be the first to admit that wasn't easy. This is where spirit came into play—a lot. There were a lot of truths I may not have wanted to acknowledge and many other surprises, too. I survived this cathartic awakening. I even surprised myself with some of the revelations.

It even dawned on me that I am way smarter than I give myself credit for! My mind and soul were beyond being book-smart. I've taken my own experiences plus the experiences of those closest to me and always learned something from them. You have to grab knowledge wherever you can get it. That's how I began absorbing everything from a very young age. I always knew I would get to the place where I needed to be. As you can see, I didn't say *wanted to be*. There is a big difference between needs and wants.

I was patient with my life, and when I let go finally, all of it came to fruition. The universe is always speaking to us. We just aren't hearing it most of the time. Hell, with social media we don't hear anything anymore. Some will say "I'm always listening," but there is a *huge* difference between hearing and listening. No one needs a tape recorder to play back everything one says. We just really want you all to really *hear* us, me included. The words *Here we are* have come to me often.

In something someone has written to me. In songs I listen to. In movies I watch. It took me a very long time to translate that and read between the lines, but I finally did. It was spirit all along telling me that they were always here with me. Here we are!

So the highly instinctual part of myself wasn't just my own intuition, it was spirit giving me the guidance. And I finally opened up to it. I mean, I can remember reoccurring dreams in my life no matter what age I was, where I remember certain numbers showing up a lot across different things. I wasn't listening this whole time. I noted them in my mind but just stored them away with other interesting things that have happened to me. Now that I know a little better, Roger made it clear to me that he was with me. The first time I was away after his passing and I returned home, I opened my apartment door and a strong force pushed me back. I remember having to take a few steps back because the feeling was so powerful. I smiled because all I could feel was calmness and joy. I said out loud "I missed you, too," and the push became even stronger. My cheeks and chin felt as if little sprinkles were touching my skin. It was a very light feeling but clearly happening. It was reminiscent of a tingly feeling. That same feeling happens all the time now, and I know it's spirit.

I mentioned being a private person before. I have been writing my entire life and very few have read my writings, which are really deep thoughts of things I've learned over time. The mind has always intrigued me, but when I put my true soul into it, all bets were off. Many folks who have read my writings have always been blown away with the breadth and depth of my soul work put into words. The time had come. I was finally ready to share my gifts with everyone. My true heart is filled with love, and many would want to dampen it, but my fear is gone. I am finally ready to show myself to the world! A beautiful man gave me the courage to tell you part of my story. And my mother has been screaming *Finally!* I realized that with telling some of my journey, I could help others going through something similar. Having love in your life is a great thing, and losing it is devastating. My journey of love and loss has different facets. My story of love and loss starts with the loss of myself. I didn't know that my heart was broken from that loss long, long ago. It took losing pure love for me to see myself clearly for the first time in my life. So, I've been grieving for what seems like a lifetime. The first thing I realized was that you can't repair yourself from a loss if you didn't know that it existed. I broke myself down with the help of a life coach and a spiritual adviser, right down to the bare bones of my soul after this realization, because I knew I wanted everything, every single thing to be clear in my life. I knew that clarity would lead to my ultimate freedom. I can't stress that enough. *Clarity!*

So, if a small part of this helps someone, that's all I can ask for. Everyone will probably experience love and loss in their lifetime, and it will never be exactly the same, but everyone should always know they aren't alone. You are never alone. You are loved. We all are loved. Again, love is universal. Spirit is with us, always. If we don't learn to truly love all on this earth, you will still have that lesson to learn—and many others when you pass on. It's not a heaven or hell thing. It's a collective-soul thing, and those with thoughts or actions that aren't generated in love will have that lesson to learn in eternity with the hope of it all finally getting through. I truly have love for everyone in my life now, and those from my past, too, because I know nothing else matters. I have love for those who weren't that kind to me in life, too. I have forgiven all of it. For some, all of this might bring them some intense revelations, but I just speak the truth of what I learned after my spiritual awakening. As humans, I think the more we share with one another, the more we can help one another. Let my experiences enrich your life in some way, and pass it all forward. Simple. As. That. A spiritual awakening is intense, and most may not think they are strong enough to handle it. Once you are wide open, there is no point in turning back.

I may have said before that we are all connected whether we like it or not. This is where loving each other should be so easy. It's all circular. My love for another should generate even more love and so on. That is the way it is meant to be. We need to stop pushing love away so much. When I have had true love in my life, things were always going to be okay. There is more of a belief of life and hope in our hearts when life is filled with love. Spreading love is not a difficult thing. This doesn't mean telling everyone you see or know that you love them all the time. It kinda means living a genuine life and helping out humankind. I give love to all things in my life; things run smoother that way. Giving a smile to someone, anyone, that can brighten their day. Just saying good morning to the cashier at Trader Joe's can give that person a moment of joy. These little things can build up and spiral into a mountain of joy. Do you see the impact love can make? Do you see the change that you can make? This is all what we are really meant to learn. We fight about love way too much, when love should be the true circulation of life.

A good friend of mine once told me that I shouldn't give my ultimate love to any man on earth. At that time, we were speaking of Ben, but in hindsight, I realized she did mean *any* man. Because I wasn't giving myself my own ultimate love and therefore not giving to God, which then entailed not giving to my source energy. See, spirit has a lot of lessons for us, but they all lead to the bottom line yet again. Love.

I'm sure you are all thinking now, what do mashed potatoes have to do with all of this? A simple thing could have more meanings, more stories, more memories attached to it than we can count. It can start out simple and become complex with so many layers to it. There are the layers again! And to be quite honest, I wanted to take things to lighter note for a minute since we have been talking through the super heavy stuff. To start this out...I love mashed potatoes! And that would include all kinds of mashed potatoes, too. Roger also loved mashed potatoes. On our very first date we ordered the same exact entrée and the exact same sides without even talking about it. We were on the same wavelength with so many things. I also can cook really good mashed potatoes. Mine are definitely the basic kind...milk, butter... like an extreme amount of butter and some salt. I hadn't had the opportunity to tell Roger that I could make really good mashed potatoes when it just slipped out one evening.

"You know, all mashed potatoes need a good gravy," he mentioned as our food arrived.

"My mashed potatoes definitely do not need gravy. They are perfect all alone," I said with extreme confidence.

The funny thing is after I said that statement, I started having extreme mashed-potatoes anxiety. And I absolutely mean that! I remember thinking...yeah, I just said that, and to add to it, I told him I felt my mashed potatoes were award-winning! When those words came out of my mouth, he lit up. That face of excitement thinking about the future and my stress levels went through the roof at the same time! I was immediately thinking, what if he didn't like my mashed potatoes? How embarrassing would that be? What if he thought they were nowhere near as good as I claimed? What if they didn't come out as good when I was going to make them for him? I went on and on in my mind. And I thought, this is what we do in life. When we are good at something, we're confident about it, but what happens when the drop of doubt seeps in and destroys all that confidence? I knew exactly how to make amazing mashed potatoes. I also wanted all the best for the man I loved. And that's why all the what-ifs crept in. If I didn't love him completely, it wouldn't have mattered to me what he thought about them.

It's crazy how memories work. I thought of Roger and this mashed-potatoes story when I was getting my hair done one day last year. I was at a new salon after more than two decades of seeing my go-to gal. So, I was looking around and just observing the new change in my life. It seemed like a lot of change was happening at once again, an apparent specialty of mine.

Ironically, there was another woman getting her hair done, and out of nowhere I overheard her discussing mashed potatoes with her hair stylist. I smiled at that point, a smile on my face, a smile in my heart. Their discussion was a little more in-depth…they were talking about these elaborate recipes. They all sounded super delicious. At that point I thought, now look how many ways there are to cook mashed potatoes. From fancy ingredients to the basics. I knew then that I had to write about this story because it brought me such joy!

I quickly jotted down the words *mashed potatoes* on a Post-it Note for later. A friend of mine saw the note and immediately thought it was maybe the beginning of a list for the grocery store. I knew those two words had an in-depth story and memory behind them. Life is as simple or complex as we make it. Some days are best simple, and others we like to bring out the parade for. That's what makes this an awesome adventure! We have to embrace both because if we don't, I feel like we are shortchanging ourselves… Did I mention that already? We have one life to live, so why not make it the best? I never had the chance to make Roger my mashed potatoes, but I know he would have loved them because he loved me. And I also know that he is laughing hysterically about this as I write it. It makes me smile when I think of it. So don't wait to make your mashed potatoes, and if they don't come out like you originally intended…I say throw in a stick of butter! That's the best advice I can give about that for now.

CHAPTER THIRTEEN

Freedom

The day I became a whole being overflowing with love, I realized that I didn't need anyone to love me: I was enough. That revelation became the key to my ultimate freedom and release. You see, I started to clear out my internal closet six years ago, and I did a damn good job with reorganizing. What I didn't know till now was that I needed to dust the cobwebs of my past going way back to the beginning. I started chapter one speaking of me not dwelling in my childhood too much. Little did I realize that was the exact place the universe wanted me to go. It makes exact sense looking at all of this in hindsight. I think it's easy to think we have moved on or healed from certain things, and then in the blink of an eye, something triggers an old, dormant wound. The wound of unworthiness was part of my foundation because it was activated early on. To watch it melt away as quickly as a cube of ice on a hot summer day was a remarkable experience. I wished that wound some love and acknowledged that it had served its purpose. "Good-bye, I don't need you here anymore. I'm surrounded by love through and through, and I wish that for you." Then I closed my eyes for a moment of silence. I put another wish out there for everyone reading this: I wish you genuine love and peace in your life. It may seem odd to some, but I thank my beautiful mother, my love Roger, and all my angels on the other side. They are the ones who brought me the strength, love, and wisdom to heal myself and find my true purpose. That is what I call spiritual leveling up!

This ultimate freedom allows my life to be so full because it is. It doesn't matter what goes on; things are just good. There are no worries because everything will be just fine. The peace is grand, and the silence is beautiful. Yes, the silence of life can be an amazing thing if you just allow it. I'm proud to have risen again in a deep meaningful way. My life is more enriched. I can see things more clearly, which still amazes me because I already had fairly clear lenses to begin with. It all just makes me smile. I feel so blessed, these words can't express the exact joy that I feel inside. The gift of my life continues, and it is the grandest thing there is. I no longer have the shackles of time or society on my back. I fluidly move day-to-day in the best form that I can. As the leader of my own life, only I know what's best; there is only one CEO, and that's me!

The day had come, the day when I finally made peace with the longest relationship of my life, my relationship with my body. All along I was adapting and changing myself for others. For what others told me I should be, what I should look like. I had lost myself long ago, and I never realized it until death hit me where it hurt the hardest. These relationships had ended in the physical, but it never dawned on me that I had ended the relationship with my true self decades before and that I had been grieving my entire life. And that was just another confirmation of the physical and spiritual all existing at once. I was in my physical body all along, yet I abused it for others and never listened to my spiritual self, which was trying to show me that I needed my own love first and foremost. It's a great feeling to say I'm healed from all the nonsense put upon me by others.

As I write the closing of this adventure, I'm smiling with such joy, for I know this is just the beginning. I'm writing an ending that talks about a beginning, and it makes total sense to me. Another birthday has passed, and was I sad? No...I was more pumped than I have ever been for another year of life. Another year of manifestation of all of my dreams. I know a new love is just around the corner, and I cannot wait. This will be the first time that I'm going into love with my heart completely filled with love as a grounded human being. I've marked my love through all its revolutions. Mark your love.